Tunisian Crochet

Tunisian Crochet

The Look of Knitting with the Ease of Crocheting

Sharon Hernes Silverman

Photographs by Alan Wycheck
Illustrations by David Bienkowski

STACKPOLE
BOOKS

Published by
STACKPOLE BOOKS
5067 Ritter Road
Mechanicsburg, PA 17055
www.stackpolebooks.com

Printed in China

10 9 8 7 6 5 4 3 2 1

First edition

All designs © Sharon Hernes Silverman, www.SharonSilverman.com
Jewelry courtesy of Patsy Keller
Cover design by Caroline M. Stover
Standard Body Measurements/Sizing, Standard Yarn Weight System, and Skill Levels
    for Crochet charts used courtesy of the Craft Yarn Council of America (CYCA),
    www.yarnstandards.com.

Library of Congress Cataloging-in-Publication Data

Silverman, Sharon Hernes.
    Tunisian crochet : the look of knitting with the ease of crocheting / Sharon Hernes
Silverman ; photographs by Alan Wycheck ; illustrations by David Bienkowski. — 1st ed.
        p. cm.
      ISBN-13: 978-0-8117-0484-7
      ISBN-10: 0-8117-0484-X
      1. Crocheting—Patterns. I. Title.
TT820.S5265   2009
746.43'4041—dc22

                                        2008030692

Contents

Acknowledgments

This book is a reality thanks to the generosity and support of many people.

I am grateful to yarn company representatives who provided supplies, encouragement, or both: Stacy Charles of Tahki • Stacy Charles, Inc.; Kristina Good, Sharon Good, and Claudia Langmaid of Unique Kolours/Colinette Yarns Ltd.; Jean Guirguis of Lion Brand Yarn Company; JoAnne Turcotte of Plymouth Yarn Company, Inc.; and Dave Van Stralen of Louet North America.

Julio DeCastro of the Henry Hanger Company of America, Inc., provided the most beautiful, high-quality products I have ever been privileged to hang something on.

The jewelry in the photographs was supplied by Patsy Keller, whose creative, exquisitely crafted designs feature stones, metal, and fused glass.

Location photos were shot at the design studio of Mary V. Knackstedt, FASID, FIIDA. Mary's interiors are instrumental in achieving the stylish look of this book.

Photographer Alan Wycheck (www.alanwycheckphoto.com) has my eternal gratitude for his preparation, patience, and creativity on this, our third book together. His ability to showcase finished items and to capture the essence of techique shots is truly an art. Despite the intensity of the photo sessions, working with Alan is always enjoyable.

Hearty thanks to David Bienkowski for taking time out from his fine art (www.art-db.com) to create crystal clear illustrations of crochet techniques.

I am grateful to Mark Allison, Editor, and Judith M. Schnell, Publisher and Vice President of Stackpole Books. Their openness and enthusiasm for this project means the world to me. Other members of the Stackpole team, Amy D. Lerner, Tracy Patterson, Donna Pope, Janelle Steen, and Caroline Stover also brought their editorial, design, marketing, and publishing expertise to this project.

Thanks to the Craft Yarn Council of America for permission to reprint charts of yarn industry standards, to the Crochet Guild of America (CGOA) for industry information and news, and to The National NeedleArts Association (TNNA) for inviting me to teach at their conference and for giving me access to top yarn industry professionals.

I appreciate the friendship and advice of knit and crochet designer Kristin Omdahl (www.styledbykristin.com). Thanks also to Anita Closic, owner of A Garden of Yarn in Chadds Ford, Pennsylvania (www.agardenofyarn.com). Anita is one of my biggest cheerleaders and is the person I turn to when I have any kind of yarn question. Her friendly, well-stocked shop is my favorite place to teach.

I could not have completed this project without the support of my friends and family. Thank you to Alan Toben for hosting me in California. Our time together was the ideal way to unwind after the TNNA conference. Babe and Seymour Hernes, Helene, Andy, and Nadine Silverman, and other family members have been unfailingly supportive of my work and life. Janet Napoli, my forever friend, has shared my excitement about this book from the beginning.

As always, love and thanks to my husband, Alan Silverman, and our sons, Jason and Steven. You guys are the best.

Introduction

Welcome to the craft of Tunisian crochet! Also known as "afghan stitch," this technique combines the best aspects of crocheting and knitting. Like crocheting, it uses a hook and the same hand motions of standard crochet; like knitting, loops are added to the hook in one direction and then worked off going the other way. Tunisian crochet uses either a long hook with a stopper on the end or a shorter hook with a long plastic extension to accommodate the many loops that will be on the hook at one time.

The results are the best of both worlds. Depending on the stitches used, Tunisian fabric appears knitted or woven, without the "loopy" look that characterizes regular crochet. Stitch combinations are almost limitless: clusters, shells, lacy openwork, and stripe patterns are just the tip of the Tunisian iceberg.

Tunisian crochet has traditionally been used for afghans and other heavy items because it can create a dense fabric. However, with the incredible variety of yarn and hooks available today, Tunisian crochet has entered the realm of high fashion. Everything from light-as-a-feather summer garments to chunky sweaters and wraps can be achieved using Tunisian crochet.

As for the origin of the terms "Tunisian crochet" and "afghan stitch," nobody is around today who can say for sure. We can only surmise that the technique may have begun in North Africa or the Near East. Whatever its genesis, today's crocheters will love the effects they can create with Tunisian crochet.

About This Book

Tunisian Crochet is designed for people who are already familiar with basic crochet stitches and are eager to add new techniques and stitch patterns to their repertoire. If you are new to crocheting, please use *Basic Crocheting: All the Skills and Tools You Need to Get Started* (Stackpole, 2006) as your introduction to the craft. Return to this book when you have mastered the essentials.

The first part of the book presents a brief review of regular crochet stitches and techniques. Next, Tunisian hooks and stitches are introduced. Step-by-step photos and detailed instructions walk you through the learning process to help you become fluent with Tunisian techniques.

The main part of the book presents sixteen projects. Designs were selected for their stylishness and variety.

Yarn and Yarn Substitutions

For each project, I chose the yarn that I thought would create the best results with the stitch pattern and shaping. You will find commercially manufactured yarn and yarn that's hand-dyed in small batches; yarn that is widely available in craft stores and yarn that is found only in specialty yarn shops; economical yarn and more expensive luxury fibers; and cotton, wool, llama, silk, metallic, and blends.

If you would like to substitute a yarn for the one specified in the pattern, choose one that is the same weight. It should also be the same style (for example, thick-and-thin) as the original yarn, but it does not need to have the same fiber content. If you prefer cotton instead of wool, for example, look for a cotton yarn that is the same weight and style of the wool. Keep in mind that the drape may be different with the new yarn.

To figure out how much you will need, calculate the total yardage using the original yarn, then calculate how many balls or skeins of your substitute yarn will give you the same yardage.

Getting Started

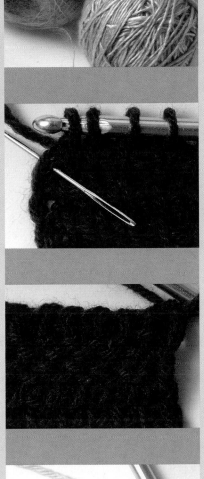

General Crochet Skills Review

Tunisian crochet builds on traditional crochet skills. This section goes over those basic techniques and stitches, step by step, in words and illustrations. If you haven't crocheted in a while, practice the basics to refresh your skills before starting a Tunisian project.

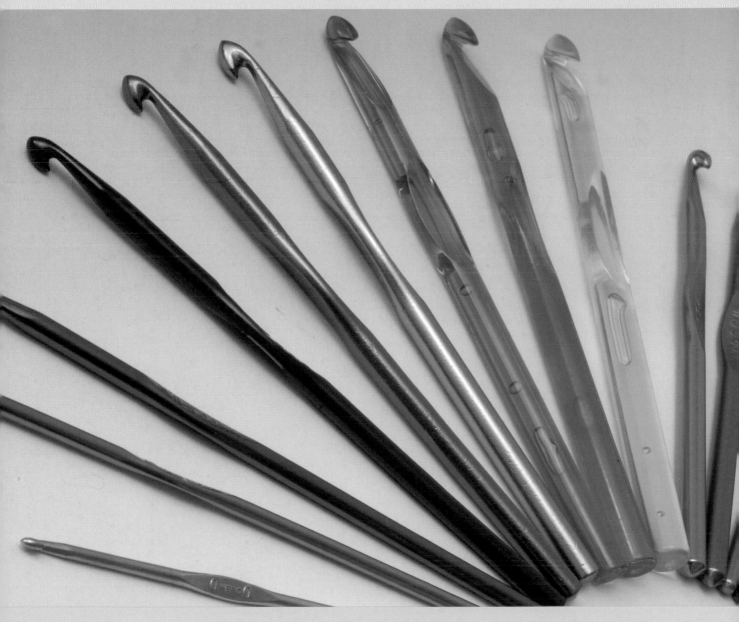

Abbreviations

Chain (ch), chains (chs)

Double crochet (dc)

Half double crochet (hdc)

Loop (lp), loops (lps)

Single crochet (sc)

Single crochet 2 together (sc2tog)

Slip stitch (sl st)

Yarn over (yo)

Chain Stitch

1. Attach yarn to hook with slip knot. Yo hook from back to front. Pull through.

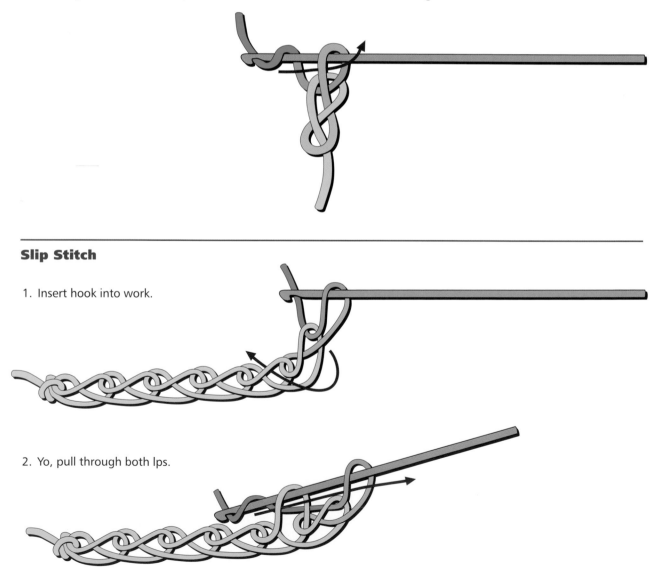

Slip Stitch

1. Insert hook into work.

2. Yo, pull through both lps.

Single Crochet

1. Insert hook into work where instructed. If you are working into the foundation ch, this will be the second ch from the hook.

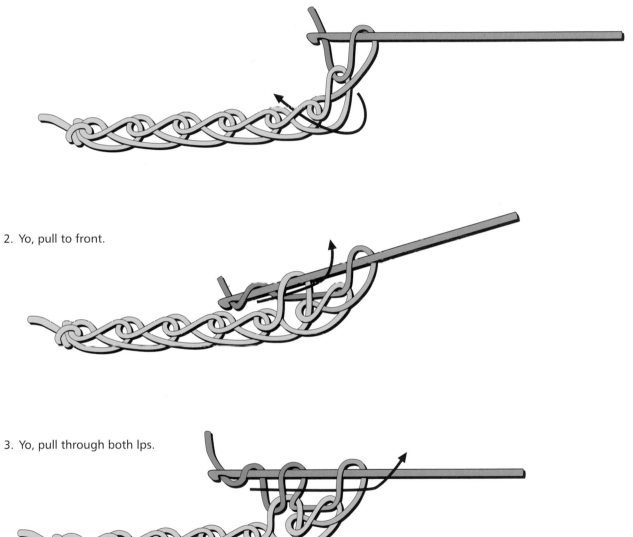

2. Yo, pull to front.

3. Yo, pull through both lps.

Half Double Crochet

1. Yo the hook. Insert into work where instructed. If you are working into the foundation ch, this will be the third ch from the hook.

2. Yo, pull to front.

3. Yo, pull through all 3 lps.

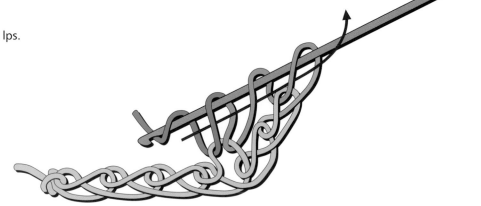

Double Crochet

1. Yo the hook. Insert into work where instructed. If you are working into the foundation ch, this will be the fourth ch from the hook.

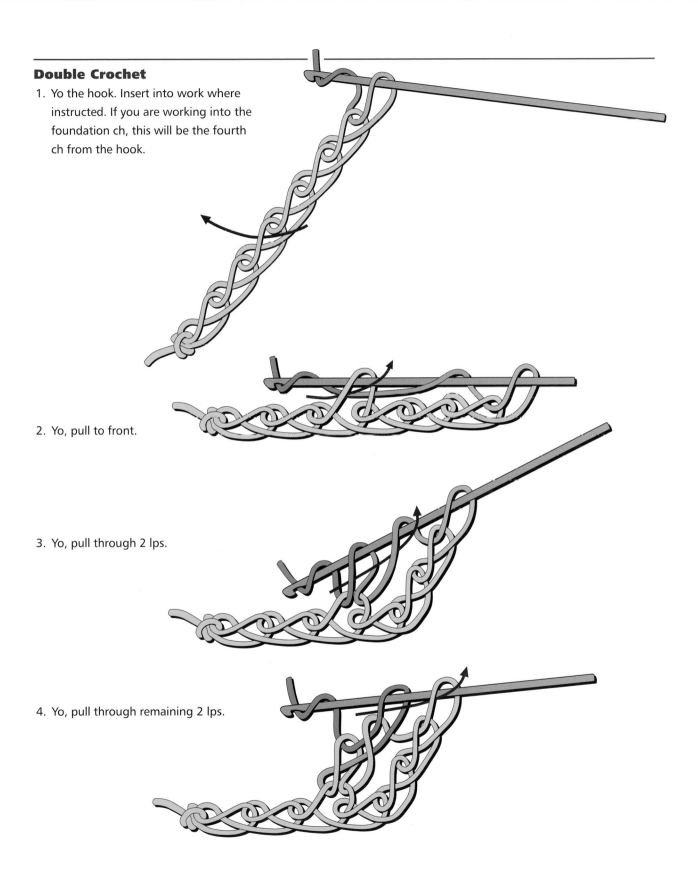

2. Yo, pull to front.

3. Yo, pull through 2 lps.

4. Yo, pull through remaining 2 lps.

Single Crochet 2 Together

This technique, also known as the single crochet decrease, is used to decrease the number of stitches, for example, around a neckline to keep it from ruffling.

1. Insert hook in next st, yo, pull up lp, 2 lps on hook.

2. Insert hook in next st, yo, pull up lp, 3 lps on hook.

3. Yo, pull through all 3 lps.

Fasten Off

Simply cut the yarn about 4 to 5 inches from the hook, yo and pull through so the tail comes through also. Pull gently to tighten. Leaving a long tail makes it easier to weave it in later with a tapestry needle.

Weave in Ends

Use a small crochet hook or a tapestry needle to weave the ends through stitches on the wrong side of your work, then clip the ends close.

Measure Gauge

Gauge is the number of stitches (or pattern repeats) and rows to a given measurement. Everyone crochets differently, so even if two people are using the same yarn, stitches, and hook, their gauges can vary.

For your work to be the right size, match the recommended gauge as closely as possible.

1. Work a swatch about 6 inches square, using the hook, yarn, and stitches specified in the pattern.
2. Block your gauge swatch to make certain that your finished item will be the desired size after it is blocked.
3. Using your gauge measurer or a rigid tape measure (not a fabric one), count the number of stitches and the number of rows you made. Compare this with the recommended gauge.

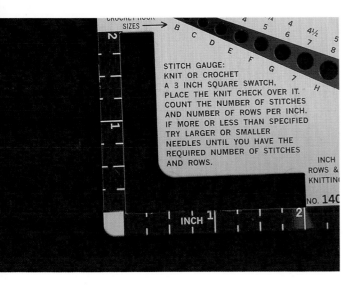

If you have more stitches or rows than you are supposed to, your gauge is too tight. Try again with a larger hook. If you have fewer rows or stitches than you are supposed to, your gauge is too loose. Try a smaller hook.

Sometimes your gauge is not equal horizontally and vertically. It is more important to match the number of stitches than the number of rows.

Blocking

Steam blocking smooths stitches, shapes a garment, squares the corners, flattens ends, and gives a professional finish.

1. Lay the item face down on a padded surface like a towel or an ironing board cover. Using stainless steel pins, pin pieces in place, shaping them into the size and shape they should be.

2. If you have a steam iron, hold it just above the crocheted pieces; the steam will set the stitches. Do not let the weight of the iron press the stitches because it will flatten them. Another alternative is to place a damp cloth on top of the items. Gently place a warm iron down on the cloth, then lift it and move it to another part of the item. Do not slide the iron around.

3. Let the pieces cool and dry before unpinning. The fabric will be nice and soft.

Tunisian Crochet Basics

Tunisian crochet has a wide assortment of stitches, each of which creates a different look. They have common elements—tools, hook action, ways to change colors, finishing methods—that are used no matter which pattern you choose. This section introduces Tunisian hooks and techniques and teaches three fundamental stitches: Tunisian simple stitch, Tunisian knit stitch, and Tunisian purl. Once you master them, you will be able to make any project in this book.

Hooks

Tunisian crochet rows are worked in two passes: The forward pass, in which loops are added to the hook, and the return pass, in which loops are worked off the hook.

Because many loops will be on the hook at one time, Tunisian crochet requires either a long hook with a stopper on the end, or a shorter hook with a flexible extension. In both cases the shaft is straight, without the thumb rest or padded handle some regular crochet hooks have. The size of the stitches is determined when they are created, so even though the plastic extension is thin, the stitches will maintain their integrity on that type of hook just like they do on a straight hook.

The hook you should use depends solely on what you find most comfortable. A straight hook tends to be heavier, because all of the stitches' weight is on that hook at once. A hook with a plastic extension is lighter, but some people do not like the way the plastic extension can flop around.

Hooks are made from many different materials, including wood, plastic, and metal. Some crocheters like the way the yarn slides on one substance better than another. Experiment with a few different hooks to see which style you prefer.

Tunisian hooks come in a wide variety of sizes, from small and delicate to the impressive size T/22 mm specimen I call the "bratwurst hook." The letter designation and millimeter size correspond to regular crochet hooks. For example, a K crochet hook and a K Tunisian hook are the same size—6.5 mm.

Some of the projects in this book use regular crochet trim; to create it, you might want to switch to a regular crochet hook in the specified size, or simply use your Tunisian hook as you would a standard hook.

Other Handy Tools

scissors or yarn cutter
tape measure
tapestry needles
pins
hook/stitch gauge measurer
steam iron or steamer
safety pins

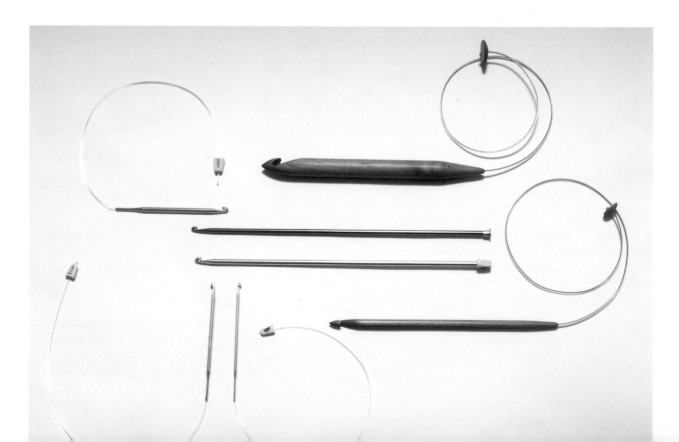

Anatomy of Tunisian Crochet

The fundamental principle of Tunisian crochet is that each row is worked in two passes: The forward pass, in which loops are added to the hook, and the return pass, in which loops are worked off the hook. The work is never turned, so the right side is always facing you.

Tunisian crochet stitches have many beautiful looks. These are achieved by different ways of inserting the hook, handling the pulled-up loops, and working off the loops.

This section teaches how to make the foundation row and execute the three basic stitches—Tunisian simple stitch, Tunisian knit stitch, and Tunisian purl stitch—that provide the basis for all other Tunisian pattern stitches. You will also learn how to work the final row of your pieces, decrease from each end, and change colors or start a new ball of yarn.

Once you have mastered these basics, you are ready to create beautiful Tunisian crochet garments, gifts, and items for the home. Each project in the book includes detailed instructions for specific stitch combinations and techniques.

Abbreviations

Chain (ch), chains (chs)
Loop (lp), loops (lps)
Skip (sk)
Stitch (st), stitches (sts)
Tunisian knit stitch (Tks)
Tunisian purl stitch (Tps)
Tunisian simple stitch (Tss)
Yarn over (yo)

Foundation Row Forward

1. Make the number of chain stitches indicated in the pattern.

> **NOTE** The number of Tunisian stitches on subsequent rows will be the same as the number of chains you start with.

Look at your chains. You may work into the top loop or into the back bump. To find the back bump, tilt the top of the chain slightly toward you. The bumps will run along the top of the row. (Some people find that working into the back bump of the foundation chain minimizes the curl that can occur in Tunisian crochet, especially with Tunisian simple stitch. If your project still curls up from the bottom, gentle steam blocking will relax that curl quite successfully.)

2. Insert hook in second ch from hook. Yo, pull up lp. There will be 2 lps on the hook.
3. Insert hook in the next ch. Yo, pull up lp. Each st adds another lp to the hook.

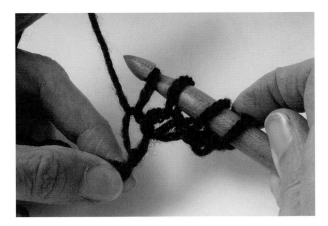

4. Continue in this fashion all the way across.
5. Count the lps. You should have the same number of lps on the hook as the number of foundation chs.

Foundation Row Return

1. Yo, pull through 1 lp.

2. Yo, pull through 2 lps.

3. Repeat Step 2 all the way across until 1 lp remains on the hook.

> **NOTE** This return method is referred to as the "standard return." When the instructions tell you to "return" or "work standard return," follow these steps. If a nonstandard return is required in a project, the pattern will provide detailed instructions.

Tunisian Simple Stitch

Work foundation row forward and return. Look at the finished stitches. You will see a vertical bar for each stitch. These bars are what you will pick up as you work the Tss forward pass.

Forward Pass

1. Sk the first vertical bar that is on the far right side, directly below the hook.

2. Put the hook from right to left through the next vertical bar. Keep the hook to the front of the work. Yo, pull up lp. There will be 2 lps on the hook.
3. Repeat Step 2 in each st across (except for far left bar), adding a lp to the hook with each st.
4. To work the final st, identify the final vertical bar and the horizontal thread that runs behind it.

Insert hook so it is behind both of those threads. This creates stability along the left side. Yo, pull up lp. Count the lps. You should have the same number as you did on the foundation row.

Return Pass

> **NOTE** This is a standard return.

1. Yo, pull through 1 lp.
2. Yo, pull through 2 lps.
3. Repeat Step 2 all the way across until 1 lp remains on hook.

After a few rows, you will see the characteristic pattern of Tunisian simple stitch.

Tunisian Knit Stitch

Work foundation row forward and return. Look at the finished stitches. Each stitch has two "legs" in an upside-down V shape.

Instead of keeping the hook to the front of the work like you did in Tss, for Tks you will poke the hook from front to back through the center of each stitch.

Forward Pass

1. Sk the first vertical bar that is on the far right side, directly below the hook.

2. Put the hook from front to back through the next st. (Stretch the stitch out slightly to see where the two vertical legs are; go right through the middle of them, not between two stitches.) Yo, pull up lp. There will be 2 lps on the hook.
3. Repeat Step 2 in each st across (except for far left bar), adding a lp to the hook with each st.
4. To work the final st, identify the final vertical bar and the horizontal thread that runs behind it.

Insert hook so it is behind both of those threads to work a Tss. Yo, pull up lp. Count the lps. You should have the same number as you did on the foundation row.

> **NOTE** Even though you are working in Tks, the final stitch is a Tss. This creates stability along the left side.

Return Pass

> **NOTE** This is a standard return.

1. Yo, pull through 1 lp.

2. Yo, pull through 2 lps.
3. Repeat Step 2 until 1 lp remains on hook.

After a few rows, you will see the characteristic pattern of Tunisian knit stitch. It looks exactly like it was knitted on two needles. The photo shows several rows of Tss followed by rows of Tks.

Tunisian Purl Stitch

Work foundation row forward and return. Look at the finished stitches. You will see a vertical bar for each stitch. These bars are what you will pick up as you work the Tps forward pass. Keep the hook to the front of the work like you did in Tss.

Forward Pass

1. Sk the first vertical bar that is on the far right side, directly below the hook. Bring the yarn to the front of the work.

2. Insert the hook into the next vertical bar, keeping the hook to the front of the work.

3. Bring the yarn toward you in front of that st, then back under the hook.

4. Yo, pull up lp.

There will be 2 lps on the hook.

5. Repeat Step 1 in each st across (except for far left bar), adding a lp to the hook with each st. Notice the "purl bump" in the front of each st.

6. To work the final st, identify the final vertical bar and the horizontal thread that runs behind it.

NOTE You will work a Tss into the final st, not a Tps. Do not move the yarn to the front of the hook.

Insert hook so it is behind both of those threads. This creates stability along the left side. Yo, pull up lp. Count the lps. You should have the same number as you did on the foundation row.

Return Pass

NOTE This is a standard return.

1. Yo, pull through 1 lp.
2. Yo, pull through 2 lps.
3. Repeat Step 2 until 1 lp remains on hook.

After a few rows, you will see the characteristic pattern of Tunisian purl stitch. It looks exactly like it was purled on two knitting needles.

Decrease in Tunisian Crochet

Sometimes you will need to decrease the number of stitches on a row in order to create shaping.

To decrease on the forward pass, work a sl st in as many stitches as are specified:

1. Insert hook into work, following the stitch pattern you have been using.

2. Yo, pull through both lps.

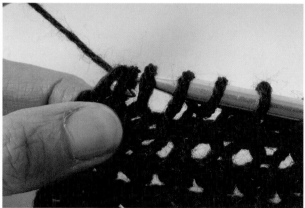

3. At the far end of the forward pass, leave stitches unworked if instructed to do so.

It is possible to decrease on the return pass. Decreasing at the beginning of the return pass is useful for armhole and shoulder shaping. Other techniques are used for decreasing evenly across a row; these are explained in project instructions.

1. Instead of yo and pull through 1 st at the beginning of the return pass, yo and pull through 2 sts.

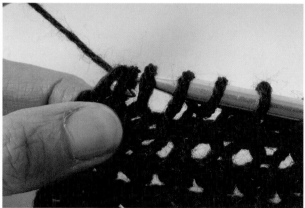

2. This creates a gentle slope. On the next forward pass, work the final stitch into that sloping final bar and the horizontal bar behind it.

Change Colors or Start New Yarn

Sometimes you will need to change colors for a stripe pattern. You will also need to start a new ball of yarn when the previous one runs out. The method is the same in both cases.

The ideal place to start a new yarn is at the end of a return pass.

1. Work return pass until 2 lps remain on hook. Drop first color to the back. Yo with new color, pull through both lps. Pull old and new tails firmly to hold stitches in place.

2. Continue working with the new yarn, making sure you are using the working end of the yarn and not the short tail.

You may also change colors at the beginning of a return pass.

1. Complete forward pass. Drop yarn to back. Lay new yarn over hook.

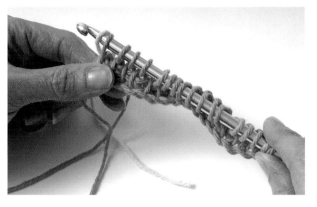

2. Begin return pass. With new yarn, yo, pull through 1 lp.

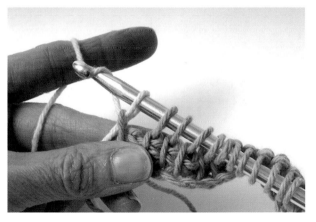

3. Continue return pass with new yarn. *Yo, pull through 2 lps. Repeat from * until 1 lp remains on hook.

Final Row

The top row of Tunisian crochet looks looser than the previous rows because nothing is worked into it. One way to end the piece neatly is to slip stitch into each stitch across the top. Insert the hook either in the space between stitch pairs or into the vertical bars like for Tunisian simple stitch, yo, pull through both lps. Since slip stitches are tight, they work best when no trim stitches will be worked into them.

If trim will be added to the final row, work single crochet stitches into each stitch across the top. Insert the hook either in the space between stitch pairs or into the vertical bars like for Tunisian simple stitch, yo, pull up a lp, yo, pull through both lps.

HELPFUL HINTS

- Never turn your work. The right side is always facing you.
- Always skip the first vertical bar.
- Pull the yarn snug at the start of each row to keep the right side from getting baggy.
- The final stitch on every forward row should be a Tunisian simple stitch, regardless of the other stitches on that row.
- Work the final stitch on the forward row into the vertical bar and the horizontal bar behind it for stability. If you turn that edge of the work toward you, it should look like a column of V-shapes marching up the side.
- Make sure you count the last stitch of the forward pass and the first stitch of the return pass separately.
- You can work any stitch into any other type of stitch (for example, Tunisian purl stitch into Tunisian knit stitch, Tunisian simple stitch into Tunisian purl stitch, and so on).
- Count! Check your stitch count regularly to make sure that you did not miss picking up a stitch on a forward pass or mistakenly pulled through too many loops on a return pass.
- To reduce the curl in Tunisian crochet, work the foundation row into the back bumps of the starting chains. To eliminate any curl that remains, gently steam block your finished items.

Projects

Chain Mail Scarf

Tunisian purl stitch is formal and structural on the front, with stitches connected to each other like the metal links in chain mail. The curly back is equally attractive, allowing you to loop, drape, sling, or wrap the scarf without regard to which side is showing.

Silk yarn worked together with very fine mohair in the same color-way creates warmth and depth without bulk.

The instructions are for a scarf that is long enough to wear folded in half with both ends comfortably pulled through the loop. For a shorter scarf, simply crochet fewer rows.

MEASUREMENTS

Finished length: 68 inches (173 centimeters),
excluding fringe

Finished width: 3.75 inches (9.5 centimeters)

MATERIALS

Colinette Tao, 100% silk, 1.75 ounces/50 grams;
128 yards/117 meters

Color: Moss (75), 2 skeins

Colinette Parisienne, 70% kid mohair, 30% polyamide,
0.88 ounces/25 grams; 241 yards/221 meters

Color: Moss (75), 1 skein

Tunisian hook size K, 6.5 mm or size needed to obtain
gauge

Crochet hook size K, 6.5 mm

Tapestry needle

8-inch piece of cardboard

GAUGE

10 Tps (Tunisian purl) stitches and 6 Tps rows/
3 inches (7.5 cm)

STITCHES AND ABBREVIATIONS

Chain stitch (ch)

Loop (lp), loops (lps)

Single crochet (sc)

Skip (sk)

Slip stitch (sl st)

Stitch (st), stitches (sts)

Tunisian purl stitch (Tps)

Tunisian simple stitch (Tss)

Yarn over (yo)

Scarf

With 1 strand of Tao and 1 strand of Parisienne held together, ch 12.

Foundation row forward: Insert hook in second ch from hook. Yo, pull up lp. 2 lps on hook. *Insert hook in next ch. Yo, pull up lp. Each st adds another lp to the hook. Repeat from * across. Total 12 lps on hook.

Return: Do not turn. Yo, pull through 1 lp. *Yo, pull through 2 lps. Repeat from * until 1 lp remains on hook.

Row 1 forward: Sk first vertical bar. *Tps in the next vertical bar. Repeat from * across to final vertical bar. Tss (not Tps) in final st, inserting hook into the vertical bar and the horizontal bar behind it for stability.

Row 1 return: Yo, pull through 1 lp. *Yo, pull through 2 lps. Repeat from * until 1 lp remains on hook.

Repeat Row 1 forward and return until scarf is approximately 67 inches (170 cm) long. Do not fasten off.

Edging

> **NOTE** The edging is worked in single crochet, starting across the top of the row just completed, then down the long side, around the bottom, and up the other side. You may use the Tunisian hook to crochet the edging or switch to the regular crochet hook.

Insert hook front-to-back into sp between first and second vertical bars. Yo, pull to front. Yo, pull through 2 lps; sc completed. Sc in each space across.

Work 2 sc in corner. If this is too tight and makes the corner curl up, add 1 more sc in corner so it is flat. Sc evenly along ends of rows down the long side. Work 2 or 3 sc in next corner. Sc evenly across bottom, around next corner, and up other long side. Work 1 or 2 sc in final corner so corner lies flat. Join to first lp with sl st. Fasten off.

Using tapestry needle, weave in ends. Gently steam block if desired.

Fringe

Each piece of fringe has 1 strand of Tao and 1 strand of Parisienne together, doubled over.

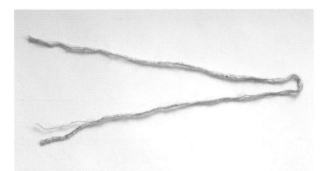

1. Using an 8-inch-long piece of cardboard, wrap yarn around 14 times, ending where you started.
2. Cut across the bottom to give 14 paired strands of equal length.
3. Fold each pair in half.
4. Using a crochet hook, pull the folded end of one pair through one corner of the scarf from front to back.
5. Pull the cut ends through the loop where the fringe is folded until the ends come through. Tighten to knot in place.

6. Place fringe every other stitch along the rest of the short end for a total of 7 fringes. Place 7 fringes on other end the same way. Trim ends. Gently steam block fringe if desired.

Wild and Woolly Wrap

This cozy quadrilateral is made from exuberant thick-and-thin yarn worked in Tunisian simple stitch. Increasing at the beginning of every row, and decreasing at the other end, creates parallel diagonal sides. Chunky tassels make a fun flourish; for a fashionable finish, use a fancy chopstick or brooch to hold the shawl closed.

Wrap yourself up in this 100 percent wool garment to stay snug and stylish at fall football games and pumpkin-picking excursions.

MEASUREMENTS

Finished width: 52 inches (132 centimeters)

Finished height: 28 inches (71 centimeters)

MATERIALS

Colinette One Zero, 100% wool, 3.5 ounces/
100 grams; 109 yards/100 meters

Color: Bright charcoal (87), 5 skeins

Tunisian hook size Q, 15.75 mm or size needed
to obtain gauge

Tapestry needle or size H crochet hook to weave
in ends

8-inch piece of cardboard

GAUGE

11 Tss/6 inches (15 cm); 5 Tss rows/4 inches (10 cm)

STITCHES AND ABBREVIATIONS

Chain stitch (ch), chain stitches (chs)

Loop (lp), loops (lps)

Tunisian simple stitch (Tss)

Skip (sk)

Space (sp)

Stitch (st), stitches (sts)

Yarn over (yo)

The challenge with thick-and-thin yarn is to make sure not to skip over the thin stitches, especially when working into the foundation chain. Practice by making 20 or 30 chains; when you make a chain with the thin part of the yarn, pull that stitch to make it a little bigger and more noticeable. Work into the chains as you would for the foundation row, counting as you go along to make sure you do not miss any stitches. This will give you the feel for working with this type of yarn.

The diagonal shape is created by increasing 1 st at the beginning of every forward row (after the foundation row), and decreasing at the beginning of each return row.

NOTE For gauge swatch, ch 20, then work in pattern until swatch measures at least 4 inches (10 cm).

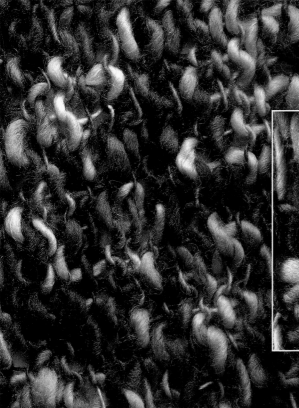

Wrap

Ch 100. When the thin part of the yarn is on the hook, be sure to keep it loose so the st will be noticeable when you work back into it.

Foundation row forward: Insert hook in second ch from hook. Yo, pull up lp. *Insert hook in next ch. Yo, pull up lp. Each st adds another lp to the hook. Repeat from * across. Total 100 lps on hook.

Return: Do not turn. Yo, pull through 1 lp. *Yo, pull through 2 lps. Repeat from * until 1 lp remains on hook.

Row 1 forward: Sk first vertical bar. Insert hook from front to back in sp between first and second vertical bars.

Yo, pull up lp. Increase made. *Tss in next vertical bar. Repeat from * across to final vertical bar. Tss in final st, inserting hook into the vertical bar and the horizontal bar behind it for stability. Total 101 lps on hook.

Row 1 return: *Yo, pull through 2 lps.

NOTE This return differs from the standard return because the first st is made by pulling through 2 lps, not 1. This decreases the number of sts by 1. The forward rows each have 101 sts, the return rows end with 100 st. This keeps the diagonal sides parallel to each other.

Repeat from * until 1 lp remains on hook.

Repeat Row 1 forward and return until wrap is approximately 27 inches.

Final row: Sk first vertical bar. Sl st in each vertical bar across. Fasten off.

Finishing

Weave in ends with tapestry needle or size H crochet hook. Gently steam block if desired.

Tassels (Make 4)

1. Cut a piece of cardboard 8 inches long. Lay a 12-inch piece of yarn across the top.

2. Starting at the bottom of the cardboard, wrap the yarn around the cardboard and over the long piece of yarn 30 times. Cut the yarn so the end is flush with the bottom of the cardboard. (Do not cut all the loops yet, just the end of the yarn you finished wrapping.)

3. Using the long piece of yarn you initially laid at the top of the cardboard, tie a knot to hold the yarn in a bundle. Do not trim yarn—you will use this to attach the tassel to the corner of the wrap.

4. Cut the yarn across the bottom of the cardboard.

5. Using a 14-inch piece of yarn, tie the bundle about 1 inch below the top. Make a nice firm knot.

6. Trim all ends of tassel, including the pieces you just used to make the knot 1 inch below the top, to the same length. (If desired, gently steam block finished tassels and retrim ends as necessary.)

7. Tie each tassel to a corner of the wrap. Put the tying yarn through several threads so it is held firmly and does not stretch the corner out of shape. Weave in those ends.

Honeycomb Skirt

Get ready for the compliments! Tunisian honeycomb stitches really show off this multicolor yarn. The skirt is designed to be flattering rather than clingy. It has a dense weave—no lining required—yet is lightweight and comfortable to wear. And speaking of weaving, many people will guess that it is woven, or perhaps knitted; they will be astonished to learn that it is crocheted.

Construction is surprisingly easy. Two identical rectangles are seamed down the sides; then an elastic waist is sewn in.

NOTES Choose the size that corresponds to your largest measurement. For example, if your waist is M and your hips are S, use instructions for M; if your waist is S and your hips are M, you would also choose M.

Pattern is written for smallest size with changes for larger sizes in parentheses. When only one number is given, it applies to all sizes. To follow pattern more easily, circle all numbers pertaining to your size before beginning.

MEASUREMENTS

Finished sizes: XS, S, M, L, XL

Finished waist: 25–26 (27–28, 29–30.5, 32–33.5, 35.5–37.3) inches [63.5–66 (68.5–71, 73.75–77.5, 81.25–85, 90.2–95.25) centimeters]

Finished hips: 35–36 (37–38, 39–40.5, 42–43.5, 45.5–47.5) inches [89–91.5 (94–96.5, 99–103, 106.75–110.5, 115.5–120.75) centimeters]

Finished length: 19 (19, 19.5, 19.5, 20) inches [48.5 (48.5, 49.5, 49.5, 50.75) centimeters]

MATERIALS

Colinette Banyan, 49% cotton, 51% viscose, 1.75 ounces/50 grams; 114 yards/104 meters

Color: Toscana (#55), 8 (9, 9, 10, 11) skeins

Tunisian hook size I, 5.5 mm or size needed to obtain gauge

Tapestry needle

Non-roll elastic, machine-washable polyester/rubber, 1 inch wide. 1 yard (0.9 meters) for sizes XS, S and M; 1.5 yards (1.35 meters) for sizes L and XL.

Sewing needle and matching thread to close casing for elastic

Two safety pins

Optional: Bodkin (a special tool designed to draw elastic through casing)

GAUGE

18 Tss/5 inches (12.5 cm); 9 honeycomb stitches (1 Tps and 1 Tss)/5 inches (12.5 cm); 9 honeycomb rows (1 Tps and 1 Tss)/4 inches (10 cm)

STITCHES AND ABBREVIATIONS

Chain stitch (ch)

Loop (lp), loops (lps)

Stitch (st), stitches (sts)

Tunisian purl stitch (Tps)

Tunisian simple stitch (Tss)

Yarn over (yo)

Honeycomb Stitch Pattern

Row 1 forward: Sk first vertical bar. *Tps in next vertical bar, Tss in next vertical bar. Repeat from * across, ending with Tss.

The photo shows a Tunisian purl stitch in progress.

Row 1 return: Yo, pull through 1 lp. *Yo, pull through 2 lps. Repeat from * untill 1 lp remains on hook.

Row 2 forward: Sk first vertical bar. *Tss in next st, Tps in next st. (The stitches are staggered: work a Tss into the Tps from the previous row, and a Tps into the Tss from the previous row. This creates the honeycomb.) When 2 sts remain, Tss into next-to-last st and final st.

Row 2 return: As Row 1 return.

Repeat Rows 1 and 2 for honeycomb pattern.

The Tunisian purl stitches have the customary "bump" of yarn crossing in front of them at the base, just like traditional purl stitches done in knitting; the Tunisian simple stitches do not.

NOTE For gauge swatch, ch 25 and work as for skirt panel until swatch measures at least 4 inches (10 cm).

Skirt Panel (Make 2)

Ch 73 (77, 83, 87, 97).

Foundation row forward: Insert hook in second ch from hook. Yo, pull up lp. *Insert hook in next ch. Yo, pull up lp. Each st adds another lp to the hook. Repeat from * across. Total 73 (77, 83, 87, 97) lps on hook.

Return: Do not turn. Yo, pull through 1 lp. *Yo, pull through 2 lps. Repeat from * until 1 lp remains on hook.

NOTE All return passes are worked this way.

Row 1: Sk first vertical bar. Tss in each vertical bar across until 1 vertical bar remains. Tss in final st, inserting hook into the vertical bar and the horizontal bar behind it for stability. Return.

Rows 2–4: Repeat Row 1.

Row 5 (commence honeycomb pattern): Sk first vertical bar. *Tps in next vertical bar, Tss in next vertical bar. Repeat from * across, ending with Tss. Return.

Row 6 (second row of honeycomb pattern): Sk first vertical bar. *Tss in next st, Tps in next st. (The stitches are staggered: you will work a Tps into the Tss from the previous row, and a Tss into the Tps from the previous row. This creates the honeycomb.) When 2 sts remain, Tss into next-to-last st and final st. Return.

Repeat Rows 5 and 6 until panel measures 18 (18, 18.25, 18.25, 19) inches [45.5 (45.5, 46.5, 46.5, 48.5) cm] from hem.

Next 11 rows: Tss forward and return. This will serve as the casing for the elastic waist.

NOTE Lay a piece of elastic on these Tss rows and make sure you can fold the waist over to cover the elastic completely and still have room to sew the waistband down over the elastic. If not, add Tss rows until you can cover the elastic.

Final row: Sk first vertical bar. Sl st into each vertical bar across. Fasten off.

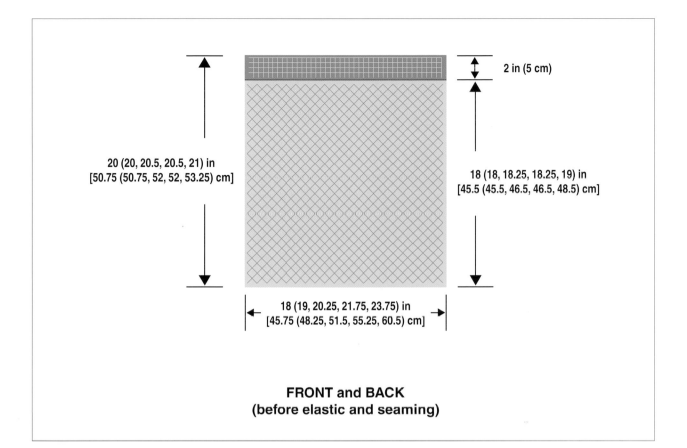

20 (20, 20.5, 20.5, 21) in
[50.75 (50.75, 52, 52, 53.25) cm]

2 in (5 cm)

18 (18, 18.25, 18.25, 19) in
[45.5 (45.5, 46.5, 46.5, 48.5) cm]

18 (19, 20.25, 21.75, 23.75) in
[45.75 (48.25, 51.5, 55.25, 60.5) cm]

FRONT and BACK
(before elastic and seaming)

Finishing

Weave in ends.

Gently steam block to size and shape.

With right sides together, use tapestry needle and yarn to sew side seams, leaving one seam's waistband casing stitches unsewn; you will feed the elastic through this spot.

Insert Elastic Waist

1. Cut elastic 2 inches (5 cm) longer than waist size. The extra length will be used for adjusting fit and finishing the ends.

2. With skirt inside out, fold casing down so final row matches up with the first Tss row.

3. Using sewing needle and matching color thread, sew bottom of casing all around. There will still be an opening at one side seam through which you will insert the elastic.

4. Pin one end of the elastic to the skirt at side seam opening so it does not disappear into the casing.

5. Feed elastic through casing. To make this easier, attach a safety pin to the end, or use a special tool called a bodkin to steer the elastic through.

6. When the elastic is all the way through, carefully unpin first end from skirt and pin ends together. (The amount of elastic used will be anywhere from 2–5 inches smaller than your waist, whatever is comfortable for you.) Check fit. Adjust length of elastic as necessary. Cut excess, leaving 1 extra inch on each end.

7. Overlap ends of elastic and stitch together firmly. Check fit one more time. Remove pin.

8. Stitch seam opening closed to completely hide elastic. Turn skirt right side out.

Shimmer Shawl

SKILL LEVEL

INTERMEDIATE

Add some "wow" to your wardrobe with this glittery wrap. Saturated colors of peacock, bronze, lilac, olive, and raspberry sparkle with gold flecks in this wonderfully dimensional yarn. The pattern alternates Tunisian double crochet stitches with a denser stitch pattern for visual interest and to keep the garment lightweight. It is finished with scallops on both short sides.

MEASUREMENTS

Finished width: 68 inches (173 centimeters)

Finished height: 24 inches (61 centimeters)

MATERIALS

Blue Heron Yarns rayon/metallic, 8 ounces/
227 grams; 550 yards/503 meters

Color: Water Hyacinth, 2 skeins

Tunisian hook size H, 5.0 mm or size needed
to obtain gauge

Crochet hook size H, 5.0 mm

Tapestry needle

GAUGE

Pattern stitch: 14 sts (sp counts as st) and
12 rows/4 inches (10 centimeters)

Tunisian double crochet: 17 sts and 4.5 rows/
5 inches (13 centimeters)

STITCHES AND ABBREVIATIONS

Chain stitch (ch)

Double crochet (dc)

Half-double crochet (hdc)

Right side (RS)

Single crochet (sc)

Skip (sk)

Slip stitch (sl st)

Space (sp), spaces (sps)

Stitch (st), stitches (sts)

Treble crochet (tr)

Tunisian double crochet (Tdc)

Tunisian simple stitch (Tss)

Wrong side (WS)

Yarn over (yo)

Special Stitch: Tunisian Double Crochet (Tdc)

Yo, insert hook into next vertical bar as for Tss,

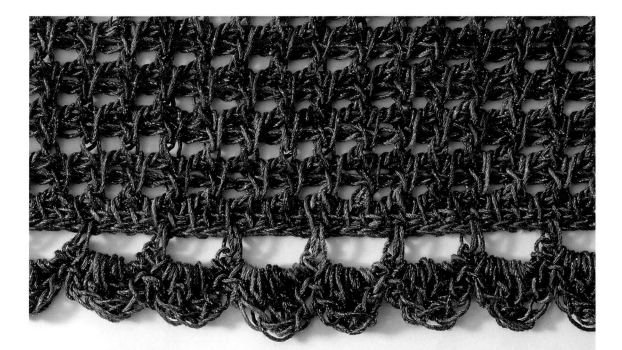

yo, pull up lp,

yo, pull through 2 lps; Tdc made.

Each st adds 1 lp to hook.

NOTE For gauge swatch, ch 26, then work in pattern until swatch measures at least 4 inches (10 cm).

Shawl

Ch 74.

Foundation row forward: Insert hook in second ch from hook. Yo, pull up lp. *Insert hook in next ch. Yo, pull up lp. Each st adds another lp to the hook. Repeat from * across. Total 74 lps on hook.

Return: Do not turn. Yo, pull through 1 lp. *Yo, pull through 2 lps. Repeat from * until 1 lp remains on hook.

NOTE All return passes are worked this way unless otherwise noted.

Row 1: Skip first vertical bar. *Insert hook in next 2 vertical bars, yo, pull through both to add 1 lp to hook,

yo to add another lp.

Repeat from * across to final vertical bar. Tss into final vertical bar and horizontal bar behind it for stability. Return.

Row 2 forward: Sk first vertical bar. Tss in next vertical bar. *Insert hook from front to back through next ch sp,

yo, pull up lp. Tss in next vertical bar. Repeat from * across to final vertical bar. Tss in final vertical bar and horizontal bar behind it. Return.

Rows 3–20: Repeat Rows 1 and 2.

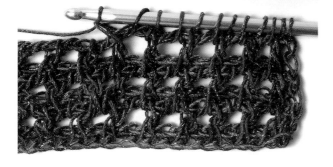

Row 21: Ch 2.

Sk first vertical bar. *Tdc in next vertical bar. Repeat from * across to final vertical bar. Tdc in final vertical bar and horizontal bar behind it. Total 74 lps on hook. Return.

Rows 22–25: Repeat Row 21.

Rows 26–45: Repeat Rows 1 and 2.

Rows 46–62: Repeat Row 21.

Rows 63–82: Repeat Rows 1 and 2.

Rows 83–87: Repeat Row 21.

Rows 88–107: Repeat Rows 1 and 2.

Row 108: Sk first vertical bar. *Insert hook in next st, yo, pull to front, yo, pull through both lps (sc made). Repeat from * across. Fasten off.

Scallop Trim (Work on Each Short Side)

NOTE Trim uses regular crochet stitches. You may use your Tunisian hook or a regular crochet hook.

Row 1: With WS facing, join yarn in corner of short side. *Ch 5. Sk 3 sts along short side. Sc in next st. Repeat from * across to corner. Total 18 ch lps.

Row 2: Ch 1. Turn to RS. *Sc, hdc, dc, tr, dc, hdc, sc in first ch loop. Repeat from * across. Fasten off.

Weave in ends.

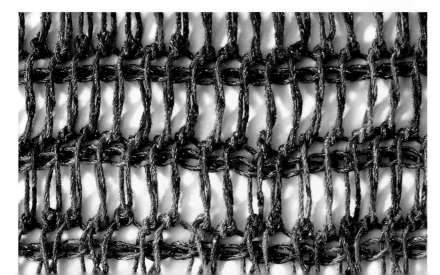

Ivory Shell

SKILL LEVEL

■■■◗

EXPERIENCED

Organic cotton yarn worked in a staggered X-stitch pattern gives this shell the color and texture of sculpted ivory. The crossed stitches create a dimensionality that catches light and shadow beautifully. A leather tie adds definition to the waist. Simple, classy, comfortable, and flattering, this shell is destined for preferred status in your wardrobe.

MEASUREMENTS

Finished sizes: XS, S, M, L

Finished chest: 32 (35, 38.5, 42) inches [81.5 (89, 98, 106.5) centimeters]

Finished length: 18 (18.25, 19, 20.5) inches [45.5 (46.5, 48.5, 52) centimeters]

NOTE Pattern is written for smallest size with changes for larger sizes in parentheses. When only one number is given, it applies to all sizes. To follow pattern more easily, circle all numbers pertaining to your size before beginning.

MATERIALS

Lion Brand Organic Cotton, 100% cotton, 1.75 ounces/50 grams; 82 yards/75 meters

Color: Almond (#002), 8 (9, 9, 10) skeins

Tunisian hook size J, 6.0 mm or size needed to obtain gauge

Crochet hook size J, 6.0 mm

Plastic stitch marker or piece of contrasting color yarn to use as marker

Tapestry needle

Leather or suede lace 56 (60, 64, 68) inches [142 (152.5, 162.5, 173) centimeters] for waist tie

GAUGE

11 stitch pairs/4 inches (10 cm) in pattern; 14 rows/ 4 inches (10 cm) in pattern

STITCHES AND ABBREVIATIONS

Chain stitch (ch)

Loop (lp), loops (lps)

Right side (RS)

Single crochet (sc)

Single crochet 2 together (sc2tog)

Slip stitch (sl st)

Stitch (st), stitches (sts)

Tunisian simple stitch (Tss)

Yarn over (yo)

Special Stitch: Single Crochet 2 Together

Insert hook in next st, yo, pull up lp, 2 lps on hook. Insert hook in next st, yo, pull up lp, 3 lps on hook, yo, pull through all 3 lps.

NOTE For gauge swatch, ch 40 and work as for back until swatch is at least 4 inches (10 cm).

Back

Ch 80 (88, 98, 108).

Foundation row forward: Insert hook in second ch from hook. Yo, pull up lp. *Insert hook in next ch. Yo, pull up lp. Each st adds another lp to the hook. Repeat from * across. Total 80 (88, 98, 108) lps on hook.

Return: Do not turn. Yo, pull through 1 lp. *Yo, pull through 2 lps. Repeat from * until 1 lp remains on hook.

Row 1 forward: Sk first vertical bar. The pattern is worked in pairs of stitches. *Insert hook in next 2 vertical bars (keeping hook to the front of work),

yo, pull up lp.

Holding just-made lp in place with your right index finger, insert hook in first vertical bar of the two bars just worked,

yo, pull up lp.

Sk second already-worked bar. Find the next pair of vertical bars. Repeat from * across to final vertical bar. Tss in final st, inserting hook into the vertical bar and the horizontal bar behind it for stability.

Row 1 return: Yo, pull through 1 lp. *Yo, pull through 2 lps. Repeat from * until 1 lp remains on hook.

NOTE All return passes are worked this way unless otherwise noted.

Row 2: Sk first vertical bar. Tss in next vertical bar. *Insert hook in next 2 vertical bars, yo, pull up lp. Holding just-made lp in place with your index finger, insert hook in first vertical bar of the two bars just worked, yo, pull up lp. Sk second already-worked bar. Find the next pair of vertical bars. Repeat from * across until two vertical bars remain. Tss into next vertical bar, Tss into final st, inserting hook into vertical bar and the horizontal bar behind it for stability. Return.

Rows 3–14: Repeat Rows 1 and 2.

Row 15: Repeat Row 1.

Row 16 (create channel for waist tie): Ch 2. Sk first 2 vertical bars, yo, Tss in next vertical bar.

*Sk next vertical bar, yo, Tss in next vertical bar. Repeat from * across. Tss into final st. 80 (88, 98, 108) lps on hook. Return.

Row 17: Tss in first sp (put hook through sp from front to back, yo, pull up lp). Tss in next vertical bar. *Tss in next sp, Tss in next vertical bar.

Repeat from * across to last st. Tss into final st. Return.
Row 18: Repeat Row 2.
Repeat Rows 1 and 2 (ending with Row 1) until piece measures 11.5 (11.75, 12, 12.5) inches [29 (30, 30.5, 32) centimeters] from bottom. Do not fasten off.

> **NOTE** This gives the garment a slight empire waist, with the tie just below the ribs. If you prefer a longer-waisted top, repeat Rows 1 and 2 (ending with Row 1) until you reach your desired length from hem to beginning of armhole.

Armhole Shaping

Row 1: Sk first vertical bar. Sl st in next vertical bar (insert hook as for Tss, yo, pull through both lps, 1 lp remains on hook). Sl st in each of next 2 vertical bars. Resume pattern, working across to last 4 vertical bars. Tss in next vertical bar. Leave last 3 vertical bars unworked. Total 74 (82, 92, 102) lps on hook. Return.

Row 2: Repeat Row 1. Total 68 (76, 86, 96) lps.

Resume pattern for 18 (18, 20, 22) additional rows.

Back of Right Shoulder Shaping

Sk first vertical bar. Work in pattern for 16 (16, 18, 20) sts. Tss in next vertical bar. Leave remaining lps unworked. Total 18 (18, 20, 22) lps on hook. Return.

Work in pattern for 2 more rows.

Last row: Sk first vertical bar. Sl st in each vertical bar across. Fasten off.

Back of Left Shoulder Shaping

Attach yarn at inner base of right shoulder in the first st that was left unworked. Pull up lp. Sl st in each vertical bar of center 32 (40, 46, 52) sts. Resume pattern, working to end of row. Total 18 (18, 20, 22) lps on hook. Return.

Work in pattern for 2 more rows.

Last row: Sk first vertical bar. Sl st in each vertical bar across. Fasten off.

Front

Work as for back to armhole shaping. Do not fasten off.

Left Front Armhole and V-Neck Shaping

Mark space after center stitch, 40 (44, 49, 54) stitches from edge, with a stitch marker or piece of contrasting color yarn. This shows the bottom of the V-neck at the exact middle of the front.

Row 1 forward: Sk first vertical bar. Sl st in each of next 3 vertical bars. Work in pattern across to st just before marker. Leave sts on other side of marker unworked. Total 37 (41, 46, 51) lps on hook.

> **NOTE** Return differs from standard return in order to create V-neck by decreasing on inner edge.

Row 1 return: *Yo, pull through 2 lps. Repeat from * across until 1 lp remains on hook.

Row 2 forward: Sk first vertical bar. Sl st in each of next 3 vertical bars. Continue in pattern until 2 sts remain. Tss in next st, Tss in final vertical bar and horizontal bar behind it (sts will be slightly slanted because of V-neck). Total 33 (37, 42, 47) lps on hook.

Row 2 return: *Yo, pull through 2 lps. Repeat from * across until 1 lp remains on hook.

Row 3 forward: Sk first vertical bar. Work in pattern across. Total 32 (36, 41, 46) lps on hook.

Row 3 return: *Yo, pull through 2 lps. Repeat from * across until 1 lp remains on hook.

Repeat Row 3 forward and return, decreasing 1 st on V-edge of each row until 18 (18, 21, 23) sts remain.

> **NOTE** This completes the V. Switch back to standard return on following rows.

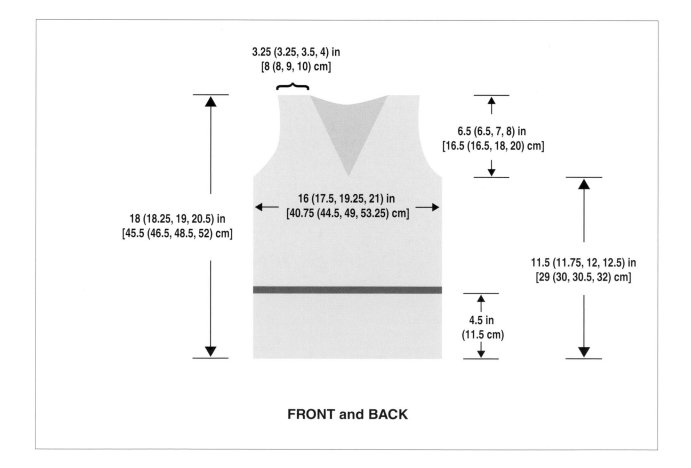

3.25 (3.25, 3.5, 4) in
[8 (8, 9, 10) cm]

6.5 (6.5, 7, 8) in
[16.5 (16.5, 18, 20) cm]

16 (17.5, 19.25, 21) in
[40.75 (44.5, 49, 53.25) cm]

18 (18.25, 19, 20.5) in
[45.5 (46.5, 48.5, 52) cm]

11.5 (11.75, 12, 12.5) in
[29 (30, 30.5, 32) cm]

4.5 in
(11.5 cm)

FRONT and BACK

Work next 6 (3, 2, 2) rows in pattern, using standard return.

Last row: Sk first vertical bar. Sl st in each vertical bar across. Fasten off.

Right Front Armhole and V-Neck Shaping

> **NOTE** Standard return on each row.

Row 1: With RS facing, join yarn in st just to left of marker. Pull up lp. Sl st in next vertical bar. Work in pattern across, leaving last 3 vertical bars unworked. Total 36 (40, 46, 50) sts on hook. Return.

Row 2: Sl st in first vertical bar to continue V-neck decrease. Work in pattern across, leaving last 3 vertical bars unworked. Total 32 (36, 42, 46) sts on hook. Return.

Row 3: Sl st in first vertical bar. Work in pattern across. Return.

Each row decreases 1 stitch along V. Repeat Row 3 until 18 (18, 21, 23) sts remain.

> **NOTE** This completes the V.

Work next 6 (3, 2, 2) rows in pattern.

Last row: Sk first vertical bar. Sl st in each vertical bar across. Fasten off.

Finishing

Weave in ends. Gently steam block to size and shape.

With right sides together, sew shoulder seams and side seams using tapestry needle and same color yarn.

Trim

> **NOTE** You can use the Tunisian crochet hook or the same size regular crochet hook for the trim. All trim is worked on the garment right side out.

Hemline Trim

Attach yarn at one seam along bottom. Ch 1. Sc evenly around bottom. Join to ch with sl st. Fasten off.

Armhole trim: Attach yarn at bottom of armhole. Ch 1. Sc in each st around armhole. Join to ch with sl st. Fasten off. Repeat for other armhole.

Neckline Trim

Row 1: Attach yarn at center back. Ch 1. Sc in each st around neck. Join to ch with sl st. Do not turn.

Row 2: Ch 1. *Sc in each of next 4 sts. Sc2tog. Repeat from * around neck, working sc2tog at bottom of V-neck. Join to ch with sl st. Fasten off.

Thread lace through channel, beginning and ending at center front. Trim lace to desired length.

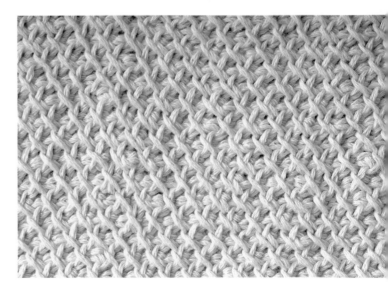

Ladders and Lattice Duster

This comfortably loose-fitting cardigan ends mid-thigh for a flattering silhouette. The linear regularity of the stitch pattern on the body makes the perfect counterpoint to the openwork sleeves. Tie it up with the crocheted belt, or let it hang open.

The sleeves are made in regular crochet from the armhole down. This method eliminates the need to seam the sleeves or to sew them to the armholes later. It also gives you the flexibility to decide on the length of the sleeves as you make them, anything from a short cap to a long bell.

MEASUREMENTS

Finished sizes: S, M, L, 1X

Finished chest: 36 (40, 44, 48) inches [91.5 (101.5, 112, 122) centimeters]

Finished length: 34.5 (35, 36.5, 37) inches [87.5 (89, 92.5, 94) centimeters]

> **NOTE** Pattern is written for smallest size with changes for larger sizes in parentheses. When only one number is given, it applies to all sizes. To follow pattern more easily, circle all numbers pertaining to your size before beginning.

MATERIALS

Lion Brand Cotton Ease, 50% cotton 50% acrylic, 3.5 ounces/50 grams; 207 yards/188 meters

Color: Violet (#191), 6 (7, 8, 9) balls

Tunisian hook size K, 6.5 mm or size needed to obtain gauge

Crochet hook size K, 6.5 mm

Crochet hook size J, 6.0 mm

Crochet hook size I, 5.5 mm

Tapestry needle

GAUGE

20 stitches (including spaces) and 12 rows in pattern/ 5 inches (13 cm)

STITCHES AND ABBREVIATIONS

Chain stitch (ch), chain stitches (chs)

Double crochet (dc)

Loop (lp), loops (lps)

Single crochet (sc)

Single crochet 2 together (sc2tog)

Skip (sk)

Slip stitch (sl st)

Stitch (st), stitches (sts)

Tunisian simple stitch (Tss)

Yarn over (yo)

Special Stitch: Single Crochet 2 Together

Insert hook in next st, yo, pull up lp, 2 lps on hook. Insert hook in next st, yo, pull up lp, 3 lps on hook, yo, pull through all 3 lps.

> **NOTE** For gauge swatch, ch 33, then work as for back until swatch measures at least 5 inches (13 cm).

Back

Ch 75 (81, 87, 93).

Foundation row forward: Insert hook in second ch from hook. Yo, pull up lp. *Insert hook in next ch. Yo, pull up lp. Each st adds another lp to the hook. Repeat from * across. Total 75 (81, 87, 93) lps on hook.

Foundation row return: Do not turn. Yo, pull through 1 lp. *Yo, pull through 2 lps. Repeat from * until 1 lp remains on hook.

NOTE All return passes are worked this way unless otherwise noted.

Row 1: Sk first vertical bar. *Tss in next vertical bar. Repeat from * across to final vertical bar. Tss in final vertical bar and the horizontal bar behind it for stability. Return.

Rows 2–3: Repeat Row 1.

Row 4 (commence pattern): Sk first vertical bar. Tss in each of next 2 vertical bars. *Yo, sk next vertical bar, Tss in next vertical bar, yo, sk next vertical bar, Tss in each of next 3 vertical bars. Repeat from * across. Return.

Rows 5–60 (5–63, 5–66, 5–68): Repeat Row 4.

Armhole Shaping

Row 1: Sk first vertical bar. Sl st in each of next 2 sts (yo, pull through 2 lps). Work in pattern across, leaving final 3 vertical bars unworked. Total 69 (75, 81, 87) lps on hook. Return.

Row 2: Repeat Row 1. Total 63 (69, 75, 81) lps on hook. Return.

Row 3: Repeat Row 1. Total 57 (63, 69, 75) lps on hook. Return.

Row 4: Repeat Row 1. Total 51 (57, 63, 69) lps on hook. Return.

Row 5 forward: Sk first vertical bar. Sl st in next vertical bar. Work pattern all the way across. Do not sk any sts at the end of the row.

Row 5 return: *Yo, pull through 2 lps. Repeat from * until 1 lp remains on hook.

NOTE This return differs from the standard return. It starts with yo, pull through 2 lps instead of yo, pull through 1 lp. This creates a decrease that matches the decrease worked by executing the sl st at the beginning of the row.

Repeat Row 5 until there are 39 (45, 51, 57) lps on hook at end of forward row. Work standard return (yo, pull through 1 lp, *yo pull through 2 lps, repeat from * until 1 lp remains on hook).

Final row: Work in pattern. Fasten off.

Right Front

Ch 39 (45, 51, 57).

Foundation row forward: Insert hook in second ch from hook. Yo, pull up lp. *Insert hook in next ch. Yo, pull up lp. Each st adds another lp to the hook. Repeat from * across. Total 39 (45, 51, 57) lps on hook.

Foundation row return: Do not turn. Yo, pull through 1 lp. *Yo, pull through 2 lps. Repeat from * until 1 lp remains on hook.

NOTE All returns are worked this way unless otherwise noted.

Row 1: Sk first vertical bar. *Tss in next vertical bar. Repeat from * across to final vertical bar. Tss in final vertical bar and the horizontal bar behind it for stability. Return.

Rows 2–3: Repeat Row 1.

Row 4 (commence pattern): Sk first vertical bar. Tss in each of next 2 vertical bars. *Yo, sk next vertical bar, Tss in next vertical bar, yo, sk next vertical bar, Tss in each of next 3 vertical bars. Repeat from * across. Return.

Rows 5–60 (5–63, 5–66, 5–68): Repeat Row 4.

Armhole Decrease and Neckline Tapering

Row 1: Sk first vertical bar. Sl st in next vertical bar. This creates the neckline shaping. Work in pattern across, leaving final 3 sts unworked. Return.

Rows 2–3: Repeat Row 1. This finishes the armhole shaping; neckline shaping continues on subsequent rows.

Row 4: Sk first vertical bar. Sl st in next vertical bar. Work in pattern across. Return.

Repeat Row 4 until there are 15 (21, 27, 36) lps on the hook at end of forward pass. Return.

Next row: Sk first vertical bar. Work in pattern across. Total 15 (21, 27, 36) lps on hook. Return.

Repeat previous row until front is same length as back. Fasten off.

Left Front

Ch 39 (45, 51, 57).

Foundation row forward: Insert hook in second ch from hook. Yo, pull up lp. *Insert hook in next ch. Yo, pull up lp. Each st adds another lp to the hook. Repeat from * across. Total 39 (45, 51, 57) lps on hook.

Foundation row return: Do not turn. Yo, pull through 1 lp. *Yo, pull through 2 lps. Repeat from * until 1 lp remains on hook.

NOTE All returns are worked this way unless otherwise noted.

Row 1: Sk first vertical bar. *Tss in next vertical bar. Repeat from * across to final vertical bar. Tss in final vertical bar and the horizontal bar behind it for stability. Return.

Rows 2–3: Repeat Row 1.

Row 4 (commence pattern): Sk first vertical bar. Tss in each of next 2 vertical bars. *Yo, sk next vertical bar, Tss in next vertical bar, yo, sk next vertical bar, Tss in each of next 3 vertical bars. Repeat from * across. Return.

Rows 5–60 (5–63, 5–66, 5–68): Repeat Row 4.

Armhole Decrease and Neckline Tapering

Row 1 forward: Sk first vertical bar. Sl st in each of next 2 vertical bars. This creates armhole shaping. Work in pattern across.

Row 1 return: *Yo, pull through 2 lps. Repeat from * until 1 lp remains on hook.

NOTE This differs from the standard return. Pulling through 2 lps at the beginning of the return pass creates the neckline tapering.

Rows 2–3: Repeat Row 1. This finishes the armhole shaping; neckline shaping continues on the return pass of subsequent rows.

Row 4 forward: Sk first vertical bar. Work in pattern across.

Row 4 return: Repeat Row 1 return.

Repeat Row 4 until there are 15 (21, 27, 36) lps on hook. Return.

NOTE This is a standard return pass, not a decrease. Yo, pull through 1 lp. *Yo, pull through 2 lps. Repeat from * until 1 lp remains on hook.

Repeat previous row until front is same length as back. Fasten off.

Finishing

Weave in ends. Gently steam block pieces to size and shape.

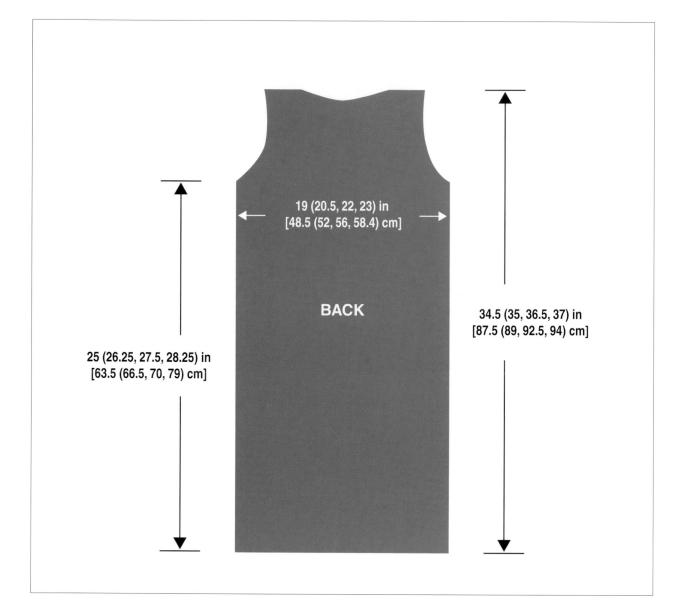

19 (20.5, 22, 23) in
[48.5 (52, 56, 58.4) cm]

BACK

34.5 (35, 36.5, 37) in
[87.5 (89, 92.5, 94) cm]

25 (26.25, 27.5, 28.25) in
[63.5 (66.5, 70, 79) cm]

Assemble Body

With right sides together, sew shoulder seams and side seams using tapestry needle and same color yarn.

Sleeve (Make 2)

NOTE Sleeve is worked in circles from the armhole down, with the garment right side out. The top and bell of the sleeve are worked with the largest crochet hook; to taper the sleeve in the center of the arm, smaller crochet hooks are used. Since the sleeve is worked from the top, you can decide on the length you want and stop when you get to that point.

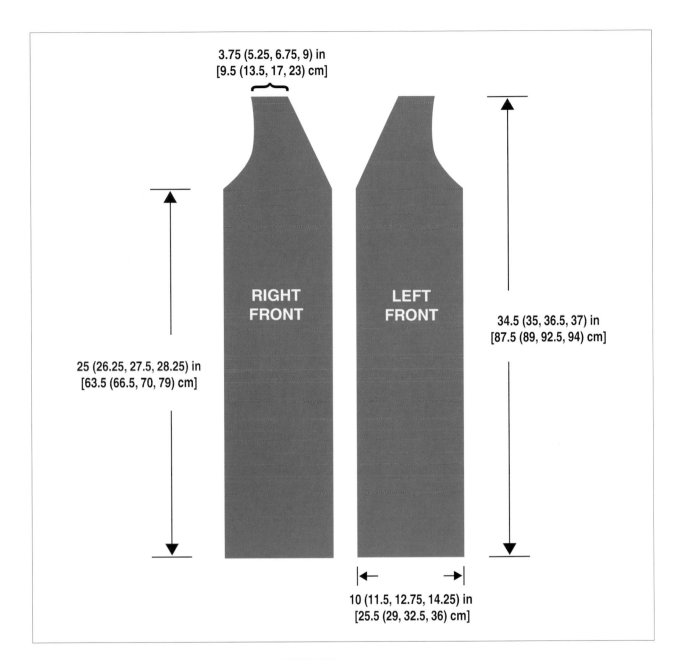

3.75 (5.25, 6.75, 9) in
[9.5 (13.5, 17, 23) cm]

RIGHT FRONT

LEFT FRONT

25 (26.25, 27.5, 28.25) in
[63.5 (66.5, 70, 79) cm]

34.5 (35, 36.5, 37) in
[87.5 (89, 92.5, 94) cm]

10 (11.5, 12.75, 14.25) in
[25.5 (29, 32.5, 36) cm]

Foundation: With regular K crochet hook, join yarn at side seam. Ch 1. Sc evenly around armhole opening. To set up for the lattice sleeve that follows, your sc stitches should be in a multiple of 4. Join to ch with sl st. Do not turn.

Round 1: Using K hook, *Ch 6. Sk 3 sc. Sc in next sc. Repeat from * around. Join to initial ch with sl st. Do not turn.

Round 2: Sc into each of first 3 ch in lattice from previous row. This will bring your hook to the top of that arch. *Ch 6. Sc into sp (around chs) at top of arch in next group of chs. Repeat from * around. Join to first ch with sl st. Do not turn.

Rounds 3–5: Repeat Round 2.

Rounds 6–10: Using J hook, repeat Round 2.

Rounds 11–20: Using I hook, repeat Round 2.

Rounds 21–25: Using J hook, repeat Round 2.

Rounds 26–30: Using K hook, repeat Round 2. Fasten off. Weave in ends.

Trim

> **NOTE** Trim is worked on the garment right side out.

Using K hook, join yarn to bottom of right front. Ch 2. Dc evenly up right front, around back of neck, and down left front. Fasten off.

Crocheted Belt

> **NOTE** Use regular crochet hook, size K. Belt is worked by creating a long chain, then sc all around.

Ch 210. Sc in second ch from hook and in each ch across. Work 4 sc at far end of ch to turn the corner. Continue sc in each ch around bottom, working 3 sc in final ch. Join to first sc with sl st. Fasten off.

Felted Clutch

Felting turns wool into matted fabric by wetting, softening, and agitating the fibers so the outer scales, or cuticles, grab onto each other. The technique—accomplished quite easily in the washing machine—works beautifully for handbags. Because the felted material shrinks the stitches and mats them together, it creates a dense fabric. There is no need to add a lining.

Any Tunisian stitch can be felted. Tunisian simple stitch looks especially nice because the texture remains visible after the fabric shrinks.

You must use wool, or a blend with a substantial wool content, if you plan to felt your project. Do not use acrylics or "nonshrinking" wool, because your goal is to shrink the piece!

This clutch uses variegated and solid-color yarn. It is worked in one piece from the top front to the bottom front, up the back, and then down again with both sides decreasing for the flap. Single crochet stitch is worked all around, and then the fabric is gently steam blocked. Side seams are sewn before felting. A decorative bead makes a secure closure.

MEASUREMENTS

Finished size of closed bag (before felting): 13 inches (33 centimeters) wide by 8 inches (20.5 centimeters) high

Finished size of closed bag (after felting): 11 inches (28 centimeters) wide by 6.5 inches (16.5 centimeters) high

MATERIALS

Lion Wool Prints (article 820), 100% wool, 2.75 ounces/78 grams; 143 yards/131 meters

Color A: Autumn Sunset (#201), 1 skein

Lion Wool Solids (article 820) 100% wool, 3 ounces/85 grams; 158 yards/144 meters

Color B: Rose (#140), 1 skein

Tunisian hook size K, 6.5 mm or size needed to obtain gauge

Crochet hook size K, 6.5 mm

1 decorative wooden bead, approximately 1 inch long

Tapestry needle

Sewing needle

Sewing thread

Safety pin

GAUGE (UNFELTED)

12 stitches and 9 rows in Tunisian simple stitch/4 inches (10 cm)

STITCHES AND ABBREVIATIONS

Chain stitch (ch)

Loop (lp), loops (lps)

Single crochet (sc)

Slip stitch (sl st)

Stitch (st), stitches (sts)

Tunisian simple stitch (Tss)

Yarn over (yo)

NOTE The handbag is made from the top front, down to the bottom and up the back, then down again for the flap.

NOTE For gauge swatch, ch 24 and work in pattern until swatch is at least 4 inches (10 cm).

Handbag

With A, ch 48.

Foundation row forward: Insert hook in second ch from hook. Yo, pull up lp. *Insert hook in next ch. Yo, pull up lp. Each st adds another lp to the hook. Repeat from * across. Total 48 lps on hook.

Foundation row return: Do not turn. Yo, pull through 1 lp. *Yo, pull through 2 lps. Repeat from * until 1 lp remains on hook.

NOTE All return passes are worked this way until the front flap decrease.

Row 1: Sk first vertical bar. *Tss in next vertical bar. Repeat from * across to final vertical bar. Tss in final vertical bar and horizontal bar behind it. Total 48 lps on hook. Return.

Rows 2–7: Repeat Row 1.

Row 8: Repeat Row 1 forward and return until 2 lps remain on hook. Drop A and let it hang to the back but do not fasten off. With B, yo and pull through 2 lps to complete return pass. Continue working in B.

Rows 9–11: Repeat Row 1 using B.

Row 12: Repeat Row 1 forward and return until there are 2 lps on hook. Drop B and let it hang to the back but do not fasten off. With A, yo and pull through 2 lps to complete return pass. Continue working in A.

NOTE Keep the yarn at the proper tension as you carry it up the back. Do not pull it too tight when you begin working with it again. Check this each time you switch colors.

Rows 13–56: Continue to work 8 rows in A and 4 rows in B until 2 lps remain on hook at the end of Row 56. Drop A but do not fasten off. With B, yo and pull through 2 lps.

Front Flap

Each row will decrease 1 st near each end. This is done by working 2 sts into 1 near the beginning of the row, and changing the way the return pass begins.

Row 57 forward: Sk first vertical bar. Put hook through next 2 vertical bars. Yo, pull through both lps (Tss decrease made). Tss in each st across to final vertical bar. Tss in final vertical bar and horizontal bar behind it. Total 47 lps on hook.

Row 57 return: *Yo, pull through 2 lps. Repeat from * across until 1 lp remains on hook.

NOTE The return differs from a standard return because the yarn is pulled through 2 lps at the beginning, not just 1 lp.

Rows 58–59: Repeat Row 57. Total 45 lps at the end of Row 58 forward, 43 st at the end of Row 59 forward.

Row 60: Repeat Row 57 forward (41 lps on hook at end of forward pass) and return until 2 lps remain on hook. Drop B. With A, yo and pull through both lps.

Rows 61–64: Work decrease rows forward and return, changing to B when 2 lps remain on hook at end of Row 64 return. Total 33 sts at end of Row 64 forward.

Rows 65–68: Work decrease rows forward and return, changing to A when 2 lps remain on hook at end of Row 68 return.

Rows 69–70: Work decrease rows forward and return, changing to B when 2 lps remain on hook at end of Row 70 return.

Rows 71–72: Work decrease rows forward and return, changing to A when 2 lps remain on hook at end of Row 72 return.

Row 73: Work decrease row forward (15 lps on hook at end of forward pass) and return, changing to B when 2 lps remain on hook at end of return.

Row 74: Work decrease row forward (13 lps on hook at end of forward pass) and return. Do not fasten off.

Stabilize Perimeter

Do not turn. Using Tunisian hook or regular crochet hook, work sc evenly around entire fabric. When you get back to the beginning, join to first sc st with a sl st. Fasten off.

Finishing

1. Cut the threads that were carried up the back about halfway between their beginning and end. Weave in ends, using tapestry needle or crochet hook.
2. Gently steam block fabric.

Assemble Bag

Fold bag so right sides are facing each other, and wrong side is out. Line up foundation row with Row 56. Use tapestry needle and B to sew one side seam, then the other. Turn right side out.

Add Loop Closure

With right side facing, attach B in center stitch of flap. Ch 8. Join with sl st to same place where you started the loop. Fasten off. Weave in ends.

Felting

1. Set washing machine to a hot wash and a cold rinse.
2. To protect the bag and the washer, insert the item into a zippered lingerie bag or pillowcase. You might want to include the handbag in a full load of wash so you do not waste water. Put bag in washer.
3. Remove handbag from washer when cycle is finished. It will look wet and a little bedraggled and may have a "wet wool" smell. These characteristics will disappear as the bag dries.

NOTE If you want the stitches to be tighter, repeat the felting process. You do not have to wait for the bag to dry (although you can refelt at that point, also).

4. Place bag on a clean, lintless towel. If necessary, put some small, clean rags into the bag to help it keep its shape as it dries.

5. Let the bag air-dry completely. Do not put it in the clothes dryer. Do not use the hair dryer. Turn the handbag over periodically so both sides dry.

Add Bead

1. Once bag is completely dry, make sure it is right side out. Position closure loop where it will be when bag is closed. With a safety pin, mark the position where the bead will be placed.

2. With sewing needle and thread, attach bead firmly to bag. Remove safety pin when bead is secure. Do not sew it too tightly or it will be hard to get the loop over the bead.

Warmhearted Vest

SKILL LEVEL

■■■□

INTERMEDIATE

The traditional shaping of this man's vest makes it an ideal layering piece with casual or dressed-up attire. Tunisian knit stitches show off the tweedy colors in a comfortable, slightly stretchy fabric. The wool yarn is soft, warm, and easy to work with.

A ribbed bottom and simple V-neck create the classic styling for this garment.

MEASUREMENTS

Finished sizes: Young man's 16 (man's S, M, L)

Finished chest: 32.5 (35, 39, 43) inches [82.5 (90, 99, 109) centimeters]

Finished length: 23 (25.5, 26.5, 27) inches [58.5 (65, 67.5, 68.5) centimeters]

> **NOTE** Pattern is written for smallest size with changes for larger sizes in parentheses. When only one number is given, it applies to all sizes. To follow pattern more easily, circle all numbers pertaining to your size before beginning.

MATERIALS

Colinette Cadenza 100% wool, 120 m/131 yds, 50 g/1.75 ounces

Color: Copperbeach (#67), 8 (9, 10, 10) skeins

Tunisian hook size J, 6.0 mm or size needed to obtain gauge

Crochet hook size I, 5.5 mm (or one size smaller than the hook you use for the main garment) for crocheting trim

Plastic stitch marker or piece of contrasting color yarn

Tapestry needle

GAUGE

17 st and 20 rows in Tunisian knit stitch/4 inches

STITCHES AND ABBREVIATIONS

Chain stitch (ch)

Loop (lp), loops (lps)

Right side (RS)

Single crochet (sc)

Single crochet 2 together (sc2tog)

Skip (sk)

Slip stitch (sl st)

Stitch (st), stitches (sts)

Tunisian knit stitch (Tks)

Tunisian purl stitch (Tps)

Tunisian simple stitch (Tss)

Yarn over (yo)

Special Stitch: Single Crochet 2 Together

Insert hook in next st, yo, pull up lp, 2 lps on hook. Insert hook in next st, yo, pull up lp, 3 lps on hook, yo, pull through all 3 lps.

> **NOTE** For gauge swatch, ch 30, then continue as for back until swatch measures at least 4 inches (10 cm).

Back

Ch 78 (84, 90, 100).

Foundation row forward: Insert hook in second ch from hook. Yo, pull up lp. *Insert hook in next ch. Yo, pull up lp. Each st adds another lp to the hook. Repeat from * across. Total 78 (84, 90, 100) lps on hook.

Return: Do not turn. Yo, pull through 1 lp. *Yo, pull through 2 lps. Repeat from * until 1 lp remains on hook.

> **NOTE** All return passes are worked this way unless otherwise noted.

Row 1 (start bottom ribbing): Sk first vertical bar. *Tps in next vertical bar, Tks in next vertical bar. Repeat from * to final vertical bar. Tss into final vertical bar and horizontal bar behind it. Return.

Rows 2–8: Repeat Row 1. The alternating knit and purl stitches create a natural ribbing.

Row 9: Sk first vertical bar. *Tks in next vertical bar. Repeat from * to final vertical bar. Tss into final vertical bar and horizontal bar behind it. Return.

Repeat Row 9 until length measures 16 (17, 18, 18) inches [40.5 (43, 45.5, 45.5) cm].

Armhole Shaping

Row 1: Sk first vertical bar. *Insert hook in next vertical bar as for Tks, yo, pull through 2 lps (sl st made). Repeat from * 7 times for total of 8 sl sts. Tks in each st across, leaving final 8 sts unworked. Total 62 (68, 74, 84) lps on hook. Return.

Row 2 forward: Sk first vertical bar. Sl st in next st. Tks in each st across to final vertical bar. Tss in final vertical bar and horizontal bar behind it. Total 61 (67, 73, 83) lps on hook.

> **NOTE** Return differs from standard return to shape armhole on that side.

Row 2 return: *Yo, pull through 2 lps. Repeat from * until 1 lp remains on hook.

Row 3 forward: Repeat Row 2 forward. Total 59 (65, 71, 81) lps on hook.

Row 3 return: Repeat Row 2 return.

Row 4 forward: Repeat Row 2 forward. Total 57 (63, 69, 79) lps on hook.

Row 4 return: Repeat Row 2 return.

> **NOTE** The armhole decrease is complete. Subsequent return passes are worked the standard way.

Row 5: Sk first vertical bar. *Tks in next st. Repeat from * across to final vertical bar. Tss in final vertical bar and horizontal bar behind it. Total 56 (62, 68, 78) lps on hook. Return.

Repeat Row 5 until back measures 6.75 (8.25, 8.25, 8.75) inches [17 (21, 21, 22) cm] from beginning of armhole decrease.

Final row: Sk first vertical bar. *Insert hook in next st as for Tks, yo, pull to front, yo, pull through 2 lps (sc made). Repeat from * in next 10 (11, 12, 12) sts. Insert hook in next st as for Tks, yo, pull through 2 lps (sl st made). Sl st in each st across until 12 (13, 14, 14) sts remain. *Insert hook in next st as for Tks, yo, pull to front, yo, pull through 2 lps (sc made). Repeat from * until final vertical bar is only st that remains. Sc in final vertical bar and horizontal bar behind it. Fasten off.

Front

Work as back to armhole shaping.

Front Left Armhole and V-neck Shaping

Set-up row for front shaping: Sk first vertical bar. *Insert hook in next vertical bar as for Tks, yo, pull through 2 lps (sl st made). Repeat from * 7 times for total of 8 sl sts. Tks in each st across, leaving final 8 sts unworked. Total 62 (68, 74, 84) lps on hook. Return.

> **NOTE** Starting with next row, stitches are only worked to the center.

Row 1 forward: Sk first vertical bar. Sl st in next st. Tks in each st across to center. Total 31 (34, 37, 42) lps on hook.

> **NOTE** Return differs from standard return to shape V-neck.

Row 1 return: *Yo, pull through 2 lps. Repeat from * until 1 lp remains on hook.

Row 2 forward: Repeat Row 2 forward until final vertical bar. Tss in final vertical bar and horizontal bar behind it (it will be on a slant from V-neck). Total 29 (32, 35, 40) lps on hook.

Row 2 return: Repeat Row 2 return.

Row 3 forward: Repeat Row 1 forward. Total 27 (30, 33, 38) lps on hook.

Row 3 return: Repeat Row 2 return.

> **NOTE** Armhole decrease is complete, but V-neck decrease on return continues.

Row 4 forward: Sk first vertical bar. *Tks in next st. Repeat from * to final vertical bar. Tss in final vertical bar and horizontal bar behind it. Total 26 (29, 32, 37) lps on hook.

Row 4 return: Repeat Row 2 return.

Repeat Row 4 forward and return until 13 (14, 15, 15) lps remain after forward pass.

Next row forward: Sk first vertical bar. Tks in each of next 11 (12, 13, 13) sts. Total 12 (13, 14, 14) lps on hook.

> **NOTE** Resume standard return here and for all subsequent return passes.

Return: Yo, pull through 1 lp. *Yo, pull through 2 lps. Repeat from * until 1 lp remains on hook.

Repeat previous row forward and return until front is same length as back.

Final row: Sk first vertical bar. Insert hook in next st as for Tks, yo, pull to front, yo, pull through 2 lps (sc made). Sc in each st across top of shoulder. Fasten off.

Front Right Armhole and V-Neck Shaping

Row 1 forward: Attach yarn at bottom center of V, in same spot where left side of V begins. Tks in each of next 30 (33, 36, 41) sts. Total 31 (34, 37, 42) lps on hook.

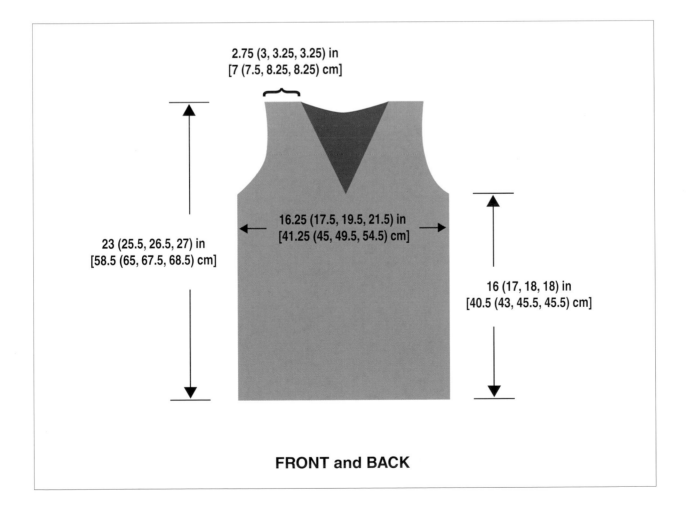

2.75 (3, 3.25, 3.25) in
[7 (7.5, 8.25, 8.25) cm]

23 (25.5, 26.5, 27) in
[58.5 (65, 67.5, 68.5) cm]

16.25 (17.5, 19.5, 21.5) in
[41.25 (45, 49.5, 54.5) cm]

16 (17, 18, 18) in
[40.5 (43, 45.5, 45.5) cm]

FRONT and BACK

NOTE Return for armhole decrease differs from standard return.

Row 1 return: *Yo, pull through 2 lps. Repeat from * until 1 lp remains on hook.

Row 2 forward: Sk first vertical bar. Sl st in next st. Tks in each of next 27 (30, 33, 38) sts. Tss in final vertical bar and horizontal bar behind it. Total 29 (32, 35, 40) lps on hook.

Row 2 return: Repeat Row 1 return.

Row 3 forward: Sk first vertical bar. Sl st in next st. Tks in each of next 25 (28, 31, 36) sts. Tss in final vertical bar and horizontal bar behind it. Total 27 (30, 33, 38) lps on hook.

Row 3 return: Repeat Row 1 return.

Row 4 forward: Sk first vertical bar. Sl st in next st. Tks in each of next 23 (26, 29, 34) sts. Tss in final vertical bar and horizontal bar behind it. Total 25 (28, 31, 36) lps on hook.

NOTE Armhole decrease is complete, so the rest of the return passes are worked in the standard way. V-neck decrease continues on forward passes with an initial sl st.

Row 4 return: Yo, pull through 1 lp. *Yo, pull through 2 lps. Repeat from * until 1 lp remains on hook.

Repeat Row 4 forward and return until 12 (13, 14, 14) lps are on hook at end of forward pass.

Next row: Sk first vertical bar. *Tks in next st. Repeat from * until final vertical bar. Tss in final vertical bar and horizontal bar behind it. Total 12 (13, 14, 14) lps on hook. Return.

Repeat previous row until front is same length as back.

Final row: Sk first vertical bar. Insert hook in next vertical bar, yo, pull to front, yo, pull through 2 lps (sc made). Sc in each st across top of shoulder. Fasten off.

Finishing

Weave in ends. Gently steam block to size and shape.

With RS together, sew shoulder seams and side seams using tapestry needle and same color yarn.

Trim

Switch to regular crochet hook (one size smaller than the Tunisian hook you used). All trim is worked on the garment with RS out.

Neckline Trim

Row 1: Join yarn at center back. Sc in each st around to bottom of V. Sc2tog at bottom. Continue working up other side to center back. Join to first st with sl st. Ch 1. Do not turn.

Row 2: *Sc in each of next 5 sts. Sc2tog. Repeat from * around. Join to ch with sl st. Fasten off.

Armhole Trim (Work Around Each Armhole)

Row 1: Join yarn at side seam. Sc evenly around. Join to first st with sl st. Ch 1. Turn.

Row 2: *Sc in each of next 5 sts. Sc2tog. Repeat from * around. Join to ch with sl st. Ch 1. Turn.

Row 3: *Sc in each of next 7 sts. Sc2tog. Repeat from * around. Join to ch with sl st. Fasten off.

Waistline Decrease

Row 1: Sk first vertical bar. Tss in next vertical bar. Sl next 2 vertical bars onto hook,

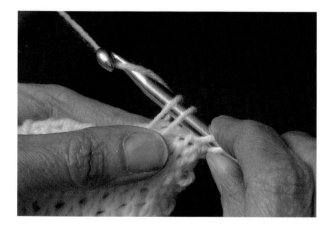

yo, pull through both to add just 1 lp onto hook. *Tss in each of next 2 sts. Sl next 2 vertical bars onto hook, yo, pull through both to add 1 lp to hook. Repeat from * across in this pattern.

> **NOTE** For sizes 18 months and 4, sl next-to-last vertical bar and final vertical bar onto hook, yo, pull through both.

Total 54 (59, 63, 68) lps on hook. Return.

Row 2: Sk first vertical bar. Tss in each of next 2 vertical bars. Sl next 2 vertical bars onto hook, yo, pull through both to add just 1 lp onto hook. *Tss in each of next 3 sts. Sl next 2 vertical bars onto hook, yo, pull through both to add 1 lp

to hook. Repeat from * across to last vertical bar. Tss in final vertical bar. Total 44 (48, 51, 55) lps on hook. Return.

Bodice

Row 1: Sk first vertical bar. *Tks in next st. Repeat from * across to final st. Tss in final st, inserting hook into vertical bar and horizontal bar behind it. Return.

Rows 2–4: Repeat Row 1.

Row 5: Repeat Row 1 forward and return until 2 lps remain on hook. Switch to B to work final return st. Let A drop to back.

Rows 6–9: Using B, repeat Row 1.

Row 10: Repeat Row 5, switching to A when 2 lps remain on hook. Let B drop to back.

Rows 11–14: Using A, repeat Row 1.

Row 15: Repeat Row 5, switching to B when 2 lps remain on hook. Let A drop to back.

Rows 16–19: Using B, repeat Row 1.

Row 20: Repeat Row 5, switching to A when 2 lps remain on hook. Let B drop to the back.

> **NOTE** Sizes 18 months and 2, skip to "Armhole Shaping" on page 71.

Rows 21–24 (sizes 4 and 6): Repeat Row 1.

Row 25 (sizes 4 and 6): Repeat Row 5, switching to B when 2 lps remain on hook. Let A drop to the back.

> **NOTE** Sizes 4 and 6, continue with "Armhole Shaping" on page 71.

Armhole Shaping

> **NOTE** All sizes, continue working 5 rows in each color, switching to other color when 2 lps remain on return pass.

Row 1: Sk first vertical bar. Sl st in each of next 3 vertical bars. Tks in each st across, leaving last 3 vertical bars unworked. Total 38 (42, 45, 49) lps on hook. Return.

Row 2: Sk first vertical bar. Sl st in next vertical bar. Tks in each st across, leaving last vertical bar unworked. Total 36 (40, 43, 47) lps on hook. Return.

Next 7 (8, 9, 10) rows: Sk first vertical bar. *Tks in next st. Repeat from * across to final vertical bar. Tss into final vertical bar and horizontal bar behind it. Total 36 (40, 43, 47) lps on hook.

> **NOTE** Remember to switch colors to maintain stripe pattern.

Back of Right Shoulder Shaping

Row 1: Sk first vertical bar. Tks in each of next 8 st, leaving rest of row unworked. Return.

Row 2: Sk first vertical bar. *Tks in next st. Repeat from * across to final vertical bar. Tss into final vertical bar and horizontal bar behind it. Total 8 lps on hook. Return.

Next 8 (9, 11, 12) rows: Repeat Row 2.

Final row: Sl st in each st across. Fasten off.

Back of Left Shoulder Shaping

Row 1: Join yarn at bottom of right shoulder shaping where the strap began. Insert hook as for Tks in next st, yo, pull to front, yo, pull through both loops (sc made). Sc over next 19 (23, 26, 30) sts. Total 20 (24, 27, 31) sc made. Tks in final 8 sts. 8 lps on hook. Return.

Row 2: Sk first vertical bar. *Tks in next st. Repeat from * across to final vertical bar. Tss into final vertical bar and horizontal bar behind it. 8 lps on hook. Return.

Next 8 (9, 11, 12) rows: Repeat Row 2.

Final row: Sl st in each st across. Fasten off.

Front

Work as back to armhole shaping. Do not fasten off.

Left Front Armhole and Neck Shaping

> **NOTE** Shaping in center is achieved on return pass.

Row 1 Forward: Sk first vertical bar. Sl st in each of next 3 vertical bars. Tks in each of next 12 sts. Total 13 lps on hook.

Row 1 Return. *Yo, pull through 2 lps. Repeat from * until 1 lp remains on hook.

> **NOTE** This differs from the standard return to shape the neckline.

Row 2 Forward: Sk first vertical bar. Sl st in next vertical bar. Tks in each of next 10 sts. Total 11 lps on hook.

Row 2 Return: Repeat Row 1 return.

Row 3 Forward: Sk first vertical bar. Tks in each of next 9 sts. Total 10 lps on hook.

Row 3 Return: Repeat Row 1 return.

Row 4 Forward: Sk first vertical bar. Tks in each of next 8 sts. Total 9 lps on hook.

Row 4 Return: Repeat Row 1 return.

Row 5: Sk first vertical bar. *Tks in next st. Repeat from * to final vertical bar. Tss in final vertical bar and horizontal bar behind it. Return.

> **NOTE** This is a standard return.

Rows 6–8 (6–9, 6–11, 6–12): Repeat Row 5.

Final row: Sl st in each st across. Fasten off.

Right Front Armhole and Neck Shaping

> **NOTE** All return passes are worked in the standard way.

Row 1: Join yarn at bottom of left side neckline, in the st following where you began the left side decrease. *In-sert hook into next st, yo, pull up lp, yo, pull through 2 lps (sc made). Repeat from * in each of next 11 sts. Total 12 sc made. Sl st in next st. Tks in each of next 11 sts. Total 12 lps on hook. Leave remaining 3 sts unworked. Return.

Row 2: Sk first vertical bar. Sl st in next st. Tks in each of next 9 sts. Total 10 lps on hook. Leave final st unworked. Return.

Row 3: Sk first vertical bar. Sl st in next st. *Tks in next st. Repeat from * across to final vertical bar. Tss in final vertical bar and horizontal bar behind it. Total 9 lps on hook. Return.

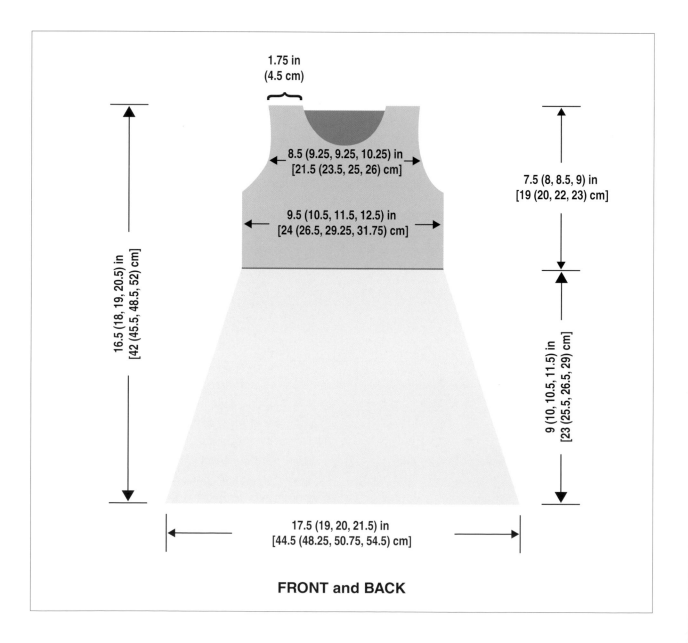

1.75 in (4.5 cm)

8.5 (9.25, 9.25, 10.25) in [21.5 (23.5, 25, 26) cm]

7.5 (8, 8.5, 9) in [19 (20, 22, 23) cm]

9.5 (10.5, 11.5, 12.5) in [24 (26.5, 29.25, 31.75) cm]

16.5 (18, 19, 20.5) in [42 (45.5, 48.5, 52) cm]

9 (10, 10.5, 11.5) in [23 (25.5, 26.5, 29) cm]

17.5 (19, 20, 21.5) in [44.5 (48.25, 50.75, 54.5) cm]

FRONT and BACK

Row 4: Sk first vertical bar. Sl st in next st. *Tks in next st. Repeat from * across to final vertical bar. Tss in final vertical bar and horizontal bar behind it. Total 8 lps on hook. Return.

Row 5: Sk first vertical bar. *Tks in next st. Repeat from * to final vertical bar. Tss in final vertical bar and horizontal bar behind it. Total 8 lps on hook. Return.

Rows 6–8 (6–9, 6–11, 6–12): Repeat Row 5.

Final row: Sl st in each st across. Fasten off.

Finishing

1. Weave in ends. Gently steam block to shape and size.
2. With right sides together, sew shoulder seams. Use a tapestry needle and the same color yarn as the top of the shoulders.
3. Still with right sides together, use a tapestry needle and Color A to sew side seams from hem to bottom of armhole.

NOTE You can use a regular crochet hook or a Tunisian hook for the trim.

Armhole Trim
(Do Around Each Armhole)

1. With dress RS out, join B at side seam.
2. Sc evenly around armhole.
3. Join to first st with sl st. Fasten off.

Neckline Trim

1. With dress RS out, join B at center back.
2. Sc evenly around neckline.

NOTE To keep neckline trim flat on the front of the neckline where the shoulder straps begin, sc2tog in each of those two spots.

3. Join to first st with sl st. Fasten off.

Hemline Trim

Row 1. With dress RS out, join B at either side seam. Sc in each st around. Join to first st with sl st. Ch 1. Turn.

Row 2 (WS): Sc in each st around. Join to ch with sl st. Ch 1. Turn.

Row 3 (RS): Sc in each st around. Join to ch with sl st. Fasten off.

Big Sister Sweater

SKILL LEVEL

◼◼◼◻

INTERMEDIATE

Yarn that's as soft as can be is used to make this raglan sleeve sweater. It's a beautiful pullover for an older girl to wear when her younger sister wears the Hug-a-li-cious Jumper.

The Tunisian net stitch, worked in the spaces between stitches, is one of my favorites. It's quick, easy, and creates a beautiful woven look that no other knit or crochet stitches can achieve. Raglan sleeves, waistline ribbing, and simple neckline trim add shape and detail to this striped pullover.

MEASUREMENTS

Finished sizes: Girl's 6 (8, 10, 12)

Finished chest: 25 (26.5, 28, 30) inches [63.5 (67, 71, 76) centimeters]

Back waist length: 10.5 (12.5, 14, 15) inches [26.5, (31.5, 35.5, 38) centimeters]

Finished cross back (shoulder to shoulder): 10.25 (10.75, 11.25, 12) inches [26 (27. 28.5, 30.5) centimeters]

Finished sleeve length to underarm: 11.5 (12.5, 13.5, 15) inches [29 (31.5, 34.5, 38) centimeters]

> **NOTE** Pattern is written for smallest size with changes for larger sizes in parentheses. When only one number is given, it applies to all sizes. To follow the pattern more easily, circle all numbers pertaining to your size before beginning.

MATERIALS

Plymouth Yarn Dreambaby D.K., 50% acrylic microfiber, 50% nylon, 1.75 ounces/50 grams; 183 yards/167 meters

Color A: Baby Blue (0102), 2 (2, 3, 3) skeins

Color B: White (0100), 4 (5, 5, 6) skeins

Tunisian hook size I, 5.5 mm or size needed to obtain gauge

Crochet hook size I, 5.5 mm

2 plastic stitch markers, or contrasting color yarn to mark stitches

Tapestry needle

GAUGE

17 stitches and 22 rows in Tunisian net stitch/4 inches (10 cm)

> **NOTE** The rows are staggered. When testing gauge, be sure to count every row, not every other row.

STITCHES AND ABBREVIATIONS

Chain stitch (ch)

Loop (lp), loops (lps)

Right side (RS)

Single crochet (sc)

Single crochet 2 together (sc2tog)

Skip (sk)

Slip stitch (sl st)

Space (sp)

Stitch (st), stitches (sts)

Tunisian knit stitch (Tks)

Tunisian net stitch (Tns)

Tunisian purl stitch (Tps)

Tunisian simple stitch (Tss)

Yarn over (yo)

Special Stitch: Single Crochet 2 Together

Insert hook in next st, yo, pull up lp, 2 lps on hook. Insert hook in next st, yo, pull up lp, 3 lps on hook, yo, pull through all 3 lps.

Special Stitch: Tunisian Net Stitch (Any Number of Ch)

Start with basic forward and return in Tss.

Row 1: Sk first 2 vertical bars. Tss into space between 2nd and 3rd sts, poking hook from front to back. Tss into each sp to final vertical bar. Tss into final vertical bar and horizontal bar behind it for stability. Return.

Row 2: Sk first vertical bar. Tss into space between 1st and 2nd vertical bars. Tss into each sp to last sp, sk last sp, Tss into final vertical bar. Return.

Repeat rows 1 and 2 for pattern.

Back

With A, ch 51 (53, 57, 61).

Foundation row forward: Insert hook in second ch from hook. Yo, pull up lp. *Insert hook in next ch. Yo, pull up lp. Each st adds another lp to the hook. Repeat from * across. Total 51 (53, 57, 61) lps on hook.

Foundation row return: Do not turn. Yo, pull through 1 lp. *Yo, pull through 2 lps. Repeat from * until 1 lp remains on hook.

NOTE All return passes are worked this way unless otherwise noted.

Row 1: Sk first vertical bar. Tps in next st. *Tks in next st, Tps in next st. Repeat from * across to final vertical bar. Tss in final vertical bar and horizontal bar behind it for stability. Total 51 (53, 57, 61) lps on hook. Return.

NOTE This begins the waistline ribbing. On rows 2–6 work Tps into Tps and Tks into Tks to maintain the rib pattern.

Rows 2–6: Repeat Row 1 until 2 lps remain on the return pass of row 6. Drop A, change to B by yo with B and pulling through final 2 bars. Continue working with B on next row.

NOTE All color changes are worked this way. Let old yarn drop to the back, pick up new color, and finish last st of return pass with new color.

Row 7: Sk first vertical bar. *Tss in next st. Repeat from * across to final vertical bar. Tss in final vertical bar and horizontal bar behind it for stability. Return.

NOTE This row of Tss sets up the Tunisian net stitch rows that follow.

Row 8 (Tunisian net stitch, Tns): Skip first 2 vertical bars. Tss into space between 2nd and 3rd sts by putting hook from front to back through that sp, yo, pull to front.

NOTE Make sure you are working between two stitches, not within a stitch.

*Tss into next sp. Repeat from * across, working 1 Tss into final sp and 1 Tss into final vertical bar and the horizontal bar behind it for stability. Total 51 (53, 57, 61) lps on hook. Return.

Row 9: Sk first vertical bar.

*Tss into next sp. Repeat from * across until 1 sp remains. Sk final sp. Tss into final vertical bar and the horizontal bar behind it for stability. Total 51 (53, 57, 61) lps on hook. Return.

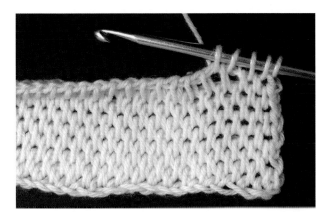

NOTE To keep the same number of lps on the hook while creating the staggered net pattern, skip the first space at the beginning of one row and do not skip any spaces at the far end of that row (you may have to look closely to find that last space). On the next row, work into the first space but skip the last space at the far end. Count your stitches to make sure you have the correct number.

Rows 10–11: Repeat Rows 8 and 9.

Continue in pattern until back measures 7.5 (9, 10.5, 11) inches [19 (23, 26.5, 28) centimeters] from beginning, changing colors at the end of the Row 14 return pass, and each 8 rows thereafter. Each color band of net stitches is 8 rows.

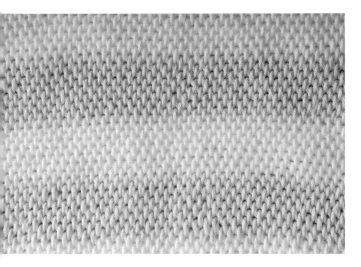

Armhole Decrease

NOTE To create the slope for raglan sleeves, a decrease is worked at both ends of each row. This is accomplished by always skipping the first two vertical bars on the forward pass, and working yo, pull through 2 lps (not 1) at the beginning of each return pass. Change colors as needed to remain in stripe pattern, with each stripe 8 rows wide.

Row 1 forward: Skip first two vertical bars. Tns across, working Tss into final vertical bar and the horizontal bar behind it for stability. Total 51 (53, 57, 61) lps on hook.

Row 1 return; *Yo, pull through 2 lps.

NOTE This differs from standard return in order to decrease at that end.

Repeat from * until 1 lp remains on hook.

Row 2 forward: Repeat Row 1. Total 50 (52, 56, 60) lps on hook.

NOTE The final vertical bar will start to slope here. Make sure you work the final st into that sloping st.

Row 2 return: Repeat Row 1 return.

Repeat Row 2 forward and return, changing colors to continue stripe pattern, until 31 (33, 35, 37) are on hook at end of forward pass. There will be 30 (32, 34, 36) pull-throughs on return.

Back Right Shoulder

Row 1: With 1 lp on hook, Tns 8 (10, 11, 11) additional sts in pattern. Total 9 (11, 12, 12) lps on hook. Leave rest of row unworked. Return.

NOTE Resume standard return here. Yo, pull through 1 lp. *Yo, pull through 2 lps. Repeat from * until 1 lp remains on hook.

Rows 2–5: Work in Tns pattern, maintaining 9 (11, 12, 12) sts on each row. Fasten off at end of Row 5 return.

Back Left Shoulder

Row 1: Sk middle 12 sts. Join yarn in next sp by putting hook through sp, yo, pull up lp. Tns 8 (10, 11, 11) sts in pattern. Total 9 (11, 12, 12) lps on hook. Return.

Rows 2–5: Work in Tns pattern, maintaining 9 (11, 12, 12) sts on each row. Fasten off at the end of Row 5 return.

Front

Work as for back through armhole decrease until 36 (38, 40, 42) lps remain on hook at end of forward pass. Return.

Left Front Neckline

> **NOTE** Continue with armhole decrease. Decrease on return to create gentle curve on neckline.

Row 1: Sk first 2 vertical bars. Work Tns in next 12 (13, 14, 14) sts, ending with 13 (14, 15, 15) lps on hook. Leave remaining sts unworked. Work return decrease.

Row 2: Repeat Row 1 forward. Total 12 (13, 14, 14) lps on hook. Work return decrease.

Repeat Row 2 until there are 9 (11, 12, 12) lps on hook at end of forward pass.

> **NOTE** Work standard return here and for rest of front (yo, pull through 1 lp, *yo, pull through 2 lps, repeat from * until 1 lp remains on hook).

Tns in pattern (alternately skipping 1 sp at the beginning of a row and the end of the following row), 9 (11, 12, 12) sts per row. Fasten off when front from base to shoulder top is same length as back.

Right Front Neckline

Row 1: Sk middle 10 bars. Rejoin yarn in next sp. Work in Tns across, ending forward row with 13 (14, 15, 15) lps on hook. Work decrease return to continue armhole decrease.

Row 2: Sk first 2 vertical bars for neckline decrease. Work Tns across. Total 12 (13, 14, 14) lps on hook. Work return decrease.

Repeat Row 2 until there are 9 (11, 12, 12) lps on hook at end of forward pass.

> **NOTE** Work standard return here and for rest of front (yo, pull through 1 lp, *yo, pull through 2 lps, repeat from * until 1 lp remains on hook).

Tns in pattern (alternately skipping 1 sp at the beginning of a row and at the end of the following row), 9 (11, 12, 12) sts per row. Fasten off when right front is same as left front.

Sleeve (Make 2)

With A, ch 29 (29, 31, 33).

Foundation row forward: Insert hook in second ch from hook. Yo, pull up lp. *Insert hook in next ch. Yo, pull up lp. Each st adds another lp to the hook. Repeat from * across. Total 29 (29, 31, 33) lps on hook.

Foundation row return: Do not turn. Yo, pull through 1 lp. *Yo, pull through 2 lps. Repeat from * until 1 lp remains on hook.

> **NOTE** All return passes are worked this way unless otherwise noted.

Row 1: Sk first vertical bar. Tps in next st. *Tks in next st, Tps in next st. Repeat from * across to final vertical bar. Tss in final vertical bar and horizontal bar behind it for stability. Total 29 (29, 31, 33) lps on hook. Return.

> **NOTE** This begins the cuff ribbing. On rows 2–6 work Tps into Tps and Tks into Tks to maintain the rib pattern.

Rows 2–6: Repeat Row 1 until 2 lps remain on the return pass of row 6. Drop A, switch to B to finish return pass. This ends the cuff ribbing. Rest of sleeve is worked in B. Cut A, leaving 6-inch tail.

Row 7: Sk first vertical bar. Tss in each st across. Total 29 (29, 31, 33) lps on hook. Return.

Row 8 (Tunisian net stitch, Tns): Skip first 2 vertical bars. Tss into space between 2nd and 3rd sts by putting hook from front to back through that sp, yo, pull to front.

> **NOTE** Make sure you are working between two stitches, not within a stitch.

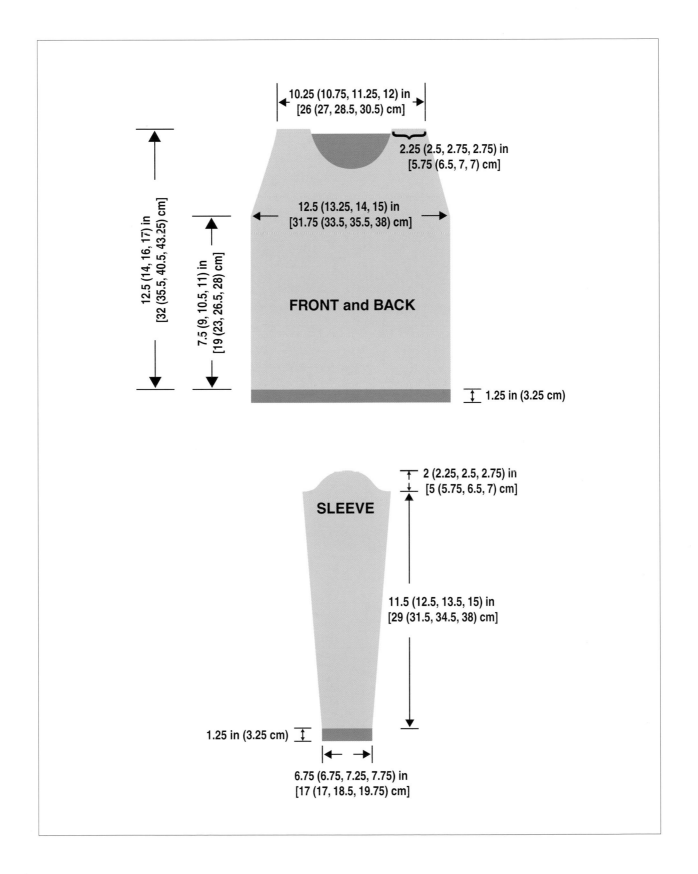

10.25 (10.75, 11.25, 12) in
[26 (27, 28.5, 30.5) cm]

2.25 (2.5, 2.75, 2.75) in
[5.75 (6.5, 7, 7) cm]

12.5 (13.25, 14, 15) in
[31.75 (33.5, 35.5, 38) cm]

12.5 (14, 16, 17) in
[32 (35.5, 40.5, 43.25) cm]

7.5 (9, 10.5, 11) in
[19 (23, 26.5, 28) cm]

FRONT and BACK

1.25 in (3.25 cm)

2 (2.25, 2.5, 2.75) in
[5 (5.75, 6.5, 7) cm]

SLEEVE

11.5 (12.5, 13.5, 15) in
[29 (31.5, 34.5, 38) cm]

1.25 in (3.25 cm)

6.75 (6.75, 7.25, 7.75) in
[17 (17, 18.5, 19.75) cm]

*Tss into next sp. Repeat from * across, working 1 Tss into final sp and 1 Tss into final vertical bar and the horizontal bar behind it. Total 29 (29, 31, 33) lps on hook. Return.

Row 9: Sk first vertical bar. *Tss into next sp. Repeat from * across until 1 sp remains. Sk final sp. Tss into final vertical bar and the horizontal bar behind it for stability. Total 29 (29, 31, 33) lps on hook. Return.

> **NOTE** To keep the same number of lps on the hook while creating the staggered net pattern, skip the first space at the beginning of one row and do not skip any spaces at the far end of that row (you may have to look closely to find that last space). On the next row, work into the first space but skip the last space at the far end. Count your stitches to make sure you have the correct number.

Rows 10–17: Repeat Rows 8 and 9.

Row 18: Repeat row 8

Row 19: Increase at end of row by working into the final space, the one that you would usually skip. Total 30 (30, 32, 34) lps on hook. Mark end of row with a stitch marker or a piece of contrasting color yarn to indicate the increase.

Work next four rows in Tns pattern.

Next row: Increase at beginning of row by working into the initial space, the one that you would usually skip. Total 31 (31, 33, 35) lps on hook. Mark beginning of row to indicate the increase.

Continue increasing in this fashion (4 rows not increase, 1 row far end increase, 4 rows not increase, 1 row near end increase) until sleeve measures 11.5 (12.5, 13.5, 15) inches. Finish with Row 9.

Sleeve Cap

Row 1 forward: Sk first two vertical bars. Work Tns across and in last space and final vertical bar.

Row 1 return (decrease return): *Yo, pull through 2 loops. Repeat from * until 1 loop remains on hook.

Repeat Row 1 forward and return until 16 (17, 18, 19) lps remain on hook at end of forward pass. Work decrease return. Fasten off.

Finishing

Weave in ends with tapestry needle. Gently steam block pieces to shape and size.

Assembly

1. With RS facing each other, sew shoulder seams. Pin sleeves in place, keeping a slight puff to the top of the shoulder. Sew sleeves to armholes.
2. Sew side seams closed. Sew sleeve seams closed.

Neckline Trim

Row 1: Turn sweater right side out. Join A at center back. Sc in each st around (sc2tog in front corners of neckline). Join to first sc with sl st. Do not turn.

Row 2: Ch 1. Sc in each sc around (sc2tog in front and back corners of neckline to keep it smooth and flat). Join to first st with sl st. Fasten off.

Toben's Pillow

SKILL LEVEL

■■□□

EASY

This gorgeous wool yarn twists tweedy roving with a fine multicolor printed strand. Worked in Tunisian simple stitch, the horizontal and vertical lines in this pillow cross to highlight the richly layered color. Reverse single crochet closes the top and bottom and results in a tailored, corded edge.

MEASUREMENTS

Finished width: 16 inches (40.5 centimeters)

Finished height: 12 inches (30.5 centimeters)

MATERIALS

Tahki Yarns Shannon, 100% wool, 1.75 ounces/
50 grams; 92 yards/85 meters

Color: Lavender multi (21), 3 skeins

12 x 16 in (30 cm x 41 cm) polyfill, washable,
nonallergenic pillow form

Tunisian hook size K, 6.5 mm or size needed to
obtain gauge

Crochet hook size K, 6.5 mm

Tapestry needle for weaving in ends

GAUGE

13 Tss stitches and 11 Tss rows/4 inches (10 cm)

STITCHES AND ABBREVIATIONS

Chain stitch (ch)

Loop (lp), loops (lps)

Reverse single crochet (rsc)

Single crochet (sc)

Slip stitch (sl st)

Stitch (st), stitches (sts)

Tunisian simple stitch (Tss)

Yarn over (yo)

Special Stitch: Reverse Single Crochet

Rsc is worked like standard sc, except the stitches go from left to right. It is also known as corded sc or crab stitch. *Insert the hook in the next st to the right. (Point the hook downwards to get it through the st more easily.) Yo, pull to front. 2 lps on hook. Yo, pull through both lps. Rsc completed. Repeat from * as indicated in pattern.

NOTE For gauge swatch, ch 30 and work as for pillow panel until swatch measures at least 4 inches (10 cm).

Pillow Panel (Make 2)

Ch 54.

Foundation row forward: Insert hook into second ch from hook. Yo, pull up lp. *Insert hook in next ch. Yo, pull up lp. Each st adds another lp to the hook. Repeat from * across. Total 54 lps on hook.

Return: Do not turn. Yo, pull through 1 lp. *Yo, pull through 2 lps. Repeat from * until 1 lp remains on hook.

Row 1 forward: Sk first vertical bar. *Tss in next vertical bar. Repeat from * across to final vertical bar. Tss in final st, inserting hook into the vertical bar and the horizontal bar behind it for stability.

Row 1 return: Yo, pull through 1 lp. *Yo, pull through 2 loops. Repeat from * until 1 lp remains on hook.

Rows 2–33: Repeat Row 1 forward and return.

Row 34: Sk first vertical bar. *Insert hook in next vertical bar. Yo, pull up lp, yo, pull through 2 lps (sc made). Repeat from * across. Fasten off.

Finishing

Weave in ends. Gently steam block both pieces to size and shape.

Close Pillow

Use a regular crochet hook or the Tunisian hook. You'll close three sides (long, short, long), then insert the pillow form and close the fourth side.

1. Place wrong sides together, right sides out.

2. Attach yarn to one corner with sc so that when you move to the right, you will be closing a long side.
3. Insert hook in next stitch to the right. Point the hook downwards to get it through the stitch more easily. Go through both thicknesses, the top and the bottom of the pillow.

4. Yo, pull up lp, yo, pull through 2 lps to complete rsc.
5. Continue working rsc in each st around 3 sides. If necessary to keep pillow flat, work 2 rsc in the corner sts.
6. Insert pillow form. Close remaining side with rsc.
7. Join final rsc to first st with sl st. Fasten off. Pull ends through to the inside to hide them.

Sweet Dreams Baby Blanket

SKILL LEVEL

INTERMEDIATE

Made with cuddly-soft, machine-washable yarn, this blanket is as practical as it is beautiful. The pattern combines crossed stitches with Tunisian knit stitches for texture and visual interest. Picot trim adds just the right finishing touch for that precious bundle.

Give the blanket for a shower or new baby gift that will be treasured for years. Nighty-night!

MEASUREMENTS

Finished width: 30 inches (76 centimeters)

Finished length: 38 inches (96.5 centimeters)

MATERIALS

Plymouth Yarn Dreambaby D.K., 50% acrylic microfiber, 50% nylon, 1.75 ounces/50 grams; 183 yards/167 meters

Color: White (100), 7 skeins

Tunisian crochet hook size J, 6.0 mm or size needed to obtain gauge

Crochet hook size J, 6.0 mm

Tapestry needle

GAUGE

18 sts and 16 rows in pattern/4 inches (10 cm)

STITCHES AND ABBREVIATIONS

Chain stitch (ch), chain stitches (chs)

Loop (lp), loops (lps)

Right side (RS)

Single crochet (sc)

Skip (sk)

Slip stitch (sl st)

Stitch (st), stitches (sts)

Tunisian knit stitch (Tks)

Tunisian simple stitch (Tss)

Wrong side (WS)

Yarn over (yo)

Stitch Pattern (Start by Chaining a Multiple of 2, Tss Forward and Return for Foundation)

The 4-row pattern alternates 2 rows of crossed Tunisian simple stitches with 2 rows of Tunisian knit stitches.

Row 1 forward: Every pair of sts, except for the first st and the last st, is worked in an X shape.

NOTE The photo shows a pair of vertical bars. You will Tss into the farther one first, then Tss into the one you skipped.

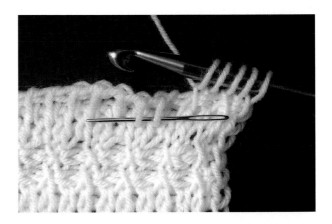

Skip first 2 vertical bars, Tss in next vertical bar. Working in front of st just made, Tss in the second skipped vertical bar (the one immediately before the one where you just made the Tss). To make it easier to find the skipped vertical bar, gently stretch the work vertically. *Move to next pair of unworked vertical bars. Sk next vertical bar, Tss in following vertical bar. Working in front of st just made, Tss in skipped vertical bar. Repeat from * to last vertical bar. Tss in last vertical bar (also picking up the horizontal strand immediately behind it for stability). Do not turn.

Row 1 return: Yo, pull through 1 lp. *Yo, pull through 2 lps. Repeat from * until 1 lp remains on hook.

NOTE All subsequent return rows are worked this way.

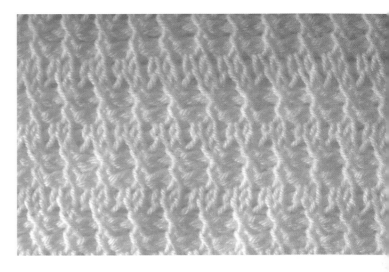

Row 2 forward and return: Repeat Row 1.

Row 3: Skip first vertical bar. Tks across to last st. Tss in final st. Return.

Row 4: Repeat Row 3.

NOTE The photo shows Row 4, the second row of Tunisian knit stitches. Note the two rows of X stitches followed by two rows of Tks.

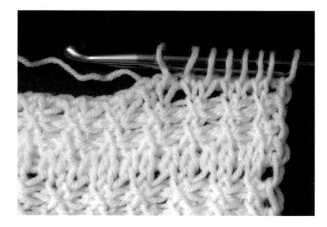

NOTE For gauge swatch, ch 36, then work in pattern until swatch measures at least 4 inches (10 cm).

Blanket

Ch 124.

Foundation row forward: Insert hook in second ch from hook. Yo, pull up lp. *Insert hook in next ch. Yo, pull up lp. Each st adds another lp to the hook. Repeat from * across. Total 124 lps on hook.

Return: Do not turn. Yo, pull through 1 lp. *Yo, pull through 2 lps. Repeat from * until 1 lp remains on hook.

Rows 1–4: Work in stitch pattern. The back (wrong side) will begin to show a series of ridges.

Rows 5–132: Repeat Rows 1–4, 32 times.

Rows 133–135: Repeat Rows 1–3.

Row 136 (finishes blanket and starts edging): You may switch to a regular crochet hook or continue to use the Tunisian hook. Sk first vertical bar. *Insert hook into next vertical bar as for Tks. Yo, pull up lp, yo, pull through 2 lps; sc made. Repeat from * across. Do not fasten off. Do not turn.

Edging

Row 1 (RS): Sc in same corner spot where final sc was made. Sc in end of each row down side. Sc 2 in corner. (If corner is too tight with 2 sc, add a third sc so it lies flat.) Sc in each st across bottom. Sc 2 in corner. Sc in end of each row up other side. Join to top corner (where you started the sc) with sl st.

Edging Row 2: Ch 1. Turn to WS. Work 1 sc in each sc around (adding sc in corners to keep flat as needed). Join to ch with sl st.

Edging Row 3 (picots): Ch 1. Turn to RS. *Sc in each of next 3 sc. Ch 3. Sl st into top of sc at base of chs to complete picot.

Repeat from * around all 4 sides. Join to first sc with sl st. Fasten off.

Weave in ends. Lightly steam block if desired.

Frosted Stitch Afghan

Llama-silk combination yarn is lightweight, warm, easy to work with, and just about shed-free. It lends itself to the Tunisian frosted stitch pattern, in which clusters like little evergreen trees alternate with formal straight-up-and-down architectural stitches.

The afghan is big enough to wrap yourself in completely. For those rare times when you're not cuddled up under it, it looks great on the family room sofa, especially when partnered with the Have It Both Ways Pillow.

MEASUREMENTS

Finished width: 44 inches (112 centimeters)

Finished length: 68 inches (173 centimeters)

MATERIALS

Plymouth Yarn Royal Llama Silk, 60% fine llama, 40% silk, 1.75 ounces/50 grams; 102 yards/ 93.25 meters

Color A, heathered brown (1001): 9 skeins

Color B, black (1572): 8 skeins

Color C, khaki (1829): 6 skeins

Tunisian crochet hook size K, 6.5 mm or size needed to obtain gauge

Crochet hook size K, 6.5 mm

Tapestry needle

GAUGE

15 sts (including spaces) and 11 rows in pattern/ 4 inches (10 cm)

STITCHES AND ABBREVIATIONS

Chain stitch (ch), chain stitches (chs)

Loop (lp), loops (lps)

Right side (RS)

Single crochet (sc)

Slip stitch (sl st)

Space (sp)

Stitch (st), stitches (sts)

Tunisian simple stitch (Tss)

Wrong side (WS)

Yarn over (yo)

To change colors, work return pass until 2 lps remain on hook. Drop first color to back. Yo with new color, pull through both lps. Use new color to work next row, pulling old and new tails firmly to hold stitches in place.

NOTE You may cut the first color, leaving at least a 4-inch tail to weave in later, or, if the old color will be used again within a few rows, simply let it hang to the back of the blanket and pick it up again when it is time to resume working with that color.

NOTE For gauge swatch, ch 33 and work in pattern until swatch is at least 4 inches (10 cm).

Afghan

Ch 141.

Foundation row forward: Insert hook in second ch from hook. Yo, pull up lp. *Insert hook in next ch. Yo, pull up lp. Each st adds another lp to the hook. Repeat from * across. Total 141 lps on hook.

Foundation row return: Do not turn. Yo, pull through 1 lp. [Yo, pull through 2 lps] twice. *Ch 1, yo, pull through 4 lps, ch 1. [Yo, pull through 2 lps] 3 times. Repeat from * until 1 lp remains on hook.

NOTE This differs from a standard return. Pulling through 4 lps where indicated creates the pointed clusters that are the hallmark of this stitch pattern.

yo, pull up lp, insert hook under next ch, yo, pull up lp. Tss into each of next 3 sts. Repeat from * across.

Row 1 return: As foundation row return.

Rows 2–7: Repeat Row 1 forward and return, changing to B when 2 lps remain on return pass.

Rows 8–13: Repeat Row 1 forward and return, changing to C when 2 lps remain on return pass.

Rows 14–27: Repeat Row 1 forward and return, changing to A when 2 lps remain on return pass.

Rows 28–36: Repeat Row 1 forward and return, changing to B when 2 lps remain on return pass.

Rows 37–50: Repeat Row 1 forward and return, changing to A when 2 lps remain on return pass.

NOTE Color pattern does not always go A, B, C. Be sure to change to color as indicated in pattern.

Rows 51–67: Repeat Row 1 forward and return, changing to C when 2 lps remain on return pass.

Rows 68–75: Repeat Row 1 forward and return, changing to B when 2 lps remain on return pass.

Rows 76–80: Repeat Row 1 forward and return, changing to A when 2 lps remain on return pass.

Rows 81–82: Repeat Row 1 forward and return, changing to B when 2 lps remain on return pass.

Rows 83–84: Repeat Row 1 forward and return, changing to A when 2 lps remain on return pass.

Rows 85–89: Repeat Row 1 forward and return, changing to B when 2 lps remain on return pass.

Row 1 forward: Sk first vertical bar. Tss in each of next 2 sts. *Insert hook under next ch, yo, pull up lp, insert hook into lp over center of cluster on previous row,

Rows 90–91: Repeat Row 1 forward and return, changing to A when 2 lps remain on return pass.

Rows 92–99: Repeat Row 1 forward and return, changing to B when 2 lps remain on return pass.

Rows 100–105: Repeat Row 1 forward and return, changing to C when 2 lps remain on return pass.

Rows 106–119: Repeat Row 1 forward and return, changing to A when 2 lps remain on return pass.

Rows 120–128: Repeat Row 1 forward and return, changing to B when 2 lps remain on return pass.

Rows 129–142: Repeat Row 1 forward and return, changing to A when 2 lps remain on return pass.

Rows 143–159: Repeat Row 1 forward and return, changing to C when 2 lps remain on return pass.

Rows 160–167: Repeat Row 1 forward and return, changing to B when 2 lps remain on return pass.

Rows 168–172: Repeat Row 1 forward and return, changing to A when 2 lps remain on return pass.

Rows 173–174: Repeat Row 1 forward and return, changing to B when 2 lps remain on return pass.

Rows 175–176: Repeat Row 1 forward and return, changing to A when 2 lps remain on return pass.

Rows 177–181: Repeat Row 1 forward and return, changing to B when 2 lps remain on return pass.

Rows 182–183: Repeat Row 1 forward and return. Do not fasten off.

Color summary:
9 rows A
6 rows B
14 rows C
9 rows A
14 rows B
17 rows A
8 rows C
5 rows B
2 rows A
2 rows B
5 rows A
2 rows B

8 rows A
6 rows B
14 rows C
9 rows A
14 rows B
17 rows A
8 rows C
5 rows B
2 rows A
2 rows B
5 rows A
2 rows B

Edging

Row 1: Do not turn (RS facing). You can use the Tunisian hook or switch to a regular crochet hook. Sc in each sp across top, 2 sc in corner (if this is too tight and makes corner curl up, work 3 sc in corner). Sc evenly down side and around rest of blanket to starting point. Join to first sc with sl st.

Row 2: Ch 1. Turn to WS. Sc evenly around, adding sc in corners as needed to keep them flat. Join to ch with sl st.

Row 3: Ch 1. Turn to RS. Sc evenly around, adding sc in corners as needed to keep them flat. Join to ch with sl st. Fasten off.

Finishing

Weave in ends. Lightly steam block.

Have It Both Ways Pillow

This pillow, made in the same khaki color that's used in the Frosted Stitch Afghan, is worked in two different stitch patterns. One side is a casual basketweave, created with the Tunisian knit and purl stitches; the other features a more formal arrangement of the same stitches, known as the plough and cable stitch. Show off front or back to suit your fancy and decor.

MEASUREMENTS

Finished size: 12 inches (30.5 cm) square

MATERIALS

Plymouth Yarn Royal Llama Silk, 60% fine llama, 40% silk, 1.75 ounces/50 grams; 102 yards/93.25meters

Color: Khaki (1829), 4 skeins

12-inch (30.5 cm) polyfill, washable, non-allergenic pillow form

Tunisian hook size I, 5.5 mm or size needed to obtain gauge

Crochet hook size I, 5.5 mm

Tapestry needle

GAUGE (BLOCKED)

For plough and cable stitch, 15 sts and 16 rows in pattern/4 inches (10 cm)

For basketweave, 4 basketweave blocks/4.5 inches (11.5 cm) horizontally; 4 basketweave blocks/4 inches (10 cm) vertically

NOTE Block your swatch before testing your gauge to ensure that the pillow panels will fit the pillow form properly. See swatch instructions on the next page for each pillow side.

STITCHES AND ABBREVIATONS

Chain stitch (ch)

Loop (lp), loops (lps)

Right side (RS)

Single crochet (sc)

Skip (sk)

Slip stitch (sl st)

Stitch (st), stitches (sts)

Tunisian knit stitch (Tks)

Tunisian purl stitch (Tps)

Tunisian simple stitch (Tss)

Yarn over (yo)

Rows 2–47: Repeat Row 1.

Row 48: Sk first vertical bar. *Insert hook in next vertical bar. Yo, pull through 2 lps. (Sl st made). Repeat from * across. Fasten off.

Plough and Cable Pillow Panel

> **NOTE** For gauge swatch, ch 28 and work as for plough and cable panel until swatch is at least 4 inches (10 cm).

Ch 44.

Foundation row forward: Insert hook into second ch from hook. Yo, pull up a loop. *Insert hook into next ch, yo, pull up a lp. Repeat from * across, adding 1 lp onto hook with each st. Total 44 lps on hook.

Foundation row return: Do not turn. Yo, pull through 1 lp. *Yo, pull through 2 lps. Repeat from * until 1 lp remains on hook.

> **NOTE** All return passes are worked this way.

Row 1 (commence pattern): Sk first vertical bar. Tss in each of next 3 sts. *Tps in each of next 4 sts. Tss in each of next 4 st. Repeat from * across, working last Tss into final vertical bar and the horizontal bar behind it for stability. Return.

Basketweave Pillow Panel

> **NOTE** For gauge swatch, ch 28 and work as for basketweave panel until swatch is at least 4 inches (10 cm).

Ch 44.

Foundation row forward: Insert hook into second ch from hook. Yo, pull up a lp. *Insert hook in next ch. Yo, pull up lp. Repeat from * across, adding 1 lp onto hook with each st. Total 44 lps on hook.

Foundation row return: Do not turn. Yo, pull through 1 lp. *Yo, pull through 2 lps. Repeat from * until 1 lp remains on hook.

> **NOTE** All return passes are worked this way.

Row 1 (commence pattern): Sk first vertical bar. Tps into each of next 3 sts. *Tks into each of next 4 sts. Tps into each of next 4 sts. Repeat from * across to last 4 vertical bars. Tps into each of next 3 vertical bars. Tss into final vertical bar and the horizontal bar behind it. Return.

Rows 2–4: Repeat Row 1.

> **NOTE** The pattern is worked for 4 rows. Knit stitches are worked into knit stitches, and purl stitches are worked into purl stitches. Then the pattern changes so that purl blocks are over knit blocks and vice versa to create the checkerboard effect. The next 3 rows again have knit over knit and purl over purl.

The only time you will work one type of stitch into the other type is on the row where the pattern changes (every 4 rows).

Row 5 (commence opposite blocks): Sk first vertical bar. Tps into each of next 3 sts. *Tks into each of next 4 sts. Tps into each of next 4 sts. Repeat from * across to final 4 vertical bars. Tks into each of next 3 vertical bars. Tss into final vertical bar and the horizontal bar behind it. Return.

Rows 6–8: Repeat Row 5.

Rows 9–12: Repeat Row 4.

Rows 13–16: Repeat Row 5.

Rows 17–20: Repeat Row 4.

Rows 21–24: Repeat Row 5.

Rows 25–28: Repeat Row 4.

Rows 29–32: Repeat Row 5.

Rows 33–36: Repeat Row 4.

Rows 37–40: Repeat Row 5.

Rows 41–43: Repeat Row 4.

Row 44: Sk first vertical bar. *Insert hook in next st. Yo, pull through 2 lps. (Sl st made.) Repeat from * across. Fasten off.

Weave in ends. Gently steam block to size and shape.

Assembly

1. With RS of panels facing each other, use tapestry needle and yarn to sew 3 sides together.
2. Turn pillow right side out. Insert pillow form.
3. Sew edges of remaining sides together. Fasten off. Using tapestry needle, pull end of yarn into pillow to hide it.

Optional Edging

To achieve a more tailored edge for the finished pillow, join yarn in any corner. Use crochet hook, size I, and sc along seam all around, working 2–3 sts in corners. Join yarn to first st with sl st. Fasten off. Using tapestry needle, pull end of yarn into pillow to hide it.

Foam Follows Function Ottoman Cover

Foam Follows Function Ottoman Cover

SKILL LEVEL

INTERMEDIATE

An inexpensive prefabricated cube or chunk of dense foam takes on new appeal dressed so uniquely! Whether you use your ottoman as a footrest, side table, or extra seat, this brightly colored ottoman cover with its huge Tunisian purl stitches adds style to any room.

Three strands of super bulky yarn are worked together to make the supersize stitches. I like the monochromatic look, but you could make each panel in a different color, or even use three different-colored strands together to create all sorts of effects.

MATERIALS

Lion Brand Wool-Ease Thick & Quick, article #640, 80% acrylic, 20% wool, 6 ounces/170 grams 108 yards/98 meters

Color: Raspberry (#112), 9 skeins

Prefabricated ottoman or rigid foam cube, 15 inches (38 centimeters) per side. (Sample is the Deluxe Memory Foam Cube Ottoman available from Overstock.com.)

Tunisian crochet hook size T (22 mm) or size needed to obtain gauge

Crochet hook size J (6 mm) or large tapestry needle for sewing panels together

Crochet hook size Q (15.75 mm) for border at bottom edge.

GAUGE

12 stitches and 9 rows in Tunisian purl stitch/ 10 inches (25.5 cm)

STITCHES AND ABBREVIATIONS

Chain stitch (ch)

Loop (lp), loops (lps)

Single crochet (sc)

Slip stitch (sl st)

Stitch (st), stitches (sts)

Tunisian purl stitch (Tps)

Tunisian simple stitch (Tss)

Yarn over (yo)

Ottoman Sides and Top (Make 5)

With 3 strands of yarn held together, ch 16.

Row 1 forward: Insert hook in second ch from hook. Yo, pull up lp. *Insert hook into next ch. Yo, pull up lp. Repeat from * across, adding a lp onto hook with each st. Total 16 lps on hook.

Row 1 return: Yo, pull through 1 lp; *yo, pull through 2 lps. Repeat from * until 1 lp remains on hook.

> **NOTE** All return passes are worked this way.

Row 2: Sk first vertical bar. *Tps in next st. Repeat from * across to final vertical bar. Tss into final vertical bar and horizontal bar behind it. Total 16 lps on hook.

> **NOTE** You can slip your left thumb under the stitch to make sure you are going under all three threads.

Return.
Rows 3–12: Repeat Row 2.

Row 13: Sk first vertical bar. Insert hook in next st as for Tss, yo, pull through 2 lps; sl st made. Sl st in each st across. Fasten off.

> **NOTE** Panel should measure 13.5 inches (34.5 centimeters) square without stretching it. This is a little smaller than one side or the top of the ottoman; the connecting stitches and the way the pieces stretch will fill in the gaps without bagging.

Border (Add to All 5 Squares)

With right side facing and using 3 strands, attach yarn in any corner. Ch 1 (this counts as first sc). Work sc in each st across top, 2 sc in corner. Continue around second, third, and fourth sides. When you get back to the beginning, work 1 sc into that corner. Join to ch with sl st. Fasten off. Weave in ends.

Join Squares

1. With RS outward, position one square on top of the ottoman. Make sure the other squares will line up so the stitches on the four sides run the same direction around the ottoman.
2. With 1 strand and a size J crochet hook (to pull yarn through sewing-fashion, not to crochet) or a large tapestry needle, whipstitch the single crochet border of each side to the corresponding sc stitches on the top, either positioning the pieces on the cube while you do this, or laying them flat.
3. Whipstitch sides together. Weave in ends.

Finish

To make bottom snug, turn ottoman upside down. With 3 strands and size Q hook, join yarn in one corner of bottom. Ch 1. Work 1 row sc all the way around. Join to ch with sl st. Fasten off.

Mardi Gras Placemats

SKILL LEVEL

■■■▢
INTERMEDIATE

Let the good times roll with this quartet of festive placemats that turn any table—indoors or out—into a party. Stripes and color changes show off some bold patterns that you can create with Tunisian stitches.

Made in machine-washable cotton, the placemats are easy to care for. Whip up a set for a gift that is sure to be used often and greatly appreciated.

MEASUREMENTS

Finished size:

17.5 inches (44.5 centimeters) wide

12.5 inches (32 centimeters) high

MATERIALS (MAKES ALL FOUR PLACEMATS):

Lion Cotton 100% cotton, 5 ounces/142 grams;
236 yards/215 meters

Color A: 148 (Turquoise), 1 skein

Color B: 157 (Sunflower), 1 skein

Color C: 147 (Purple), 1 skein

Color D: 108 (Morning Glory Blue) 108, 1 skein

Tunisian hook size J (6 mm) or size needed to
obtain gauge

Crochet hook size J (6 mm)

Tapestry needle

GAUGE

See instructions for each placemat for the proper
gauge

STITCHES AND ABBREVIATIONS

Chain stitch (ch)

Loop (lp), loops (lps)

Slip (sl)

Slip stitch (sl st)

Stitch (st), stitches (sts)

Tunisian simple stitch (Tss)

Yarn over (yo)

Tricolor Stripe

GAUGE

15 sts in Tunisian simple stitch/4 inches (10 cm); 16
rows in Tunisian simple stitch/5 inches (13 cm)

NOTE For gauge swatch, ch 30, then work in
pattern until swatch measures at least 5 inches
(13 cm).

With A, ch 46.

Foundation row forward: Insert hook in second ch from hook. Yo, pull up lp. *Insert hook in next ch. Yo, pull up lp. Each st adds another lp to the hook. Repeat from * across. Total 46 loops on hook. Drop A by letting it hang to back.

Return: Switch to B by laying yarn on hook and starting to work with it.

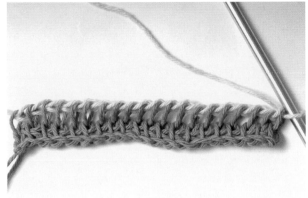

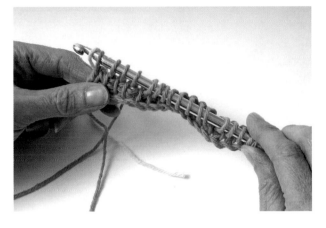

Yo, pull through 1 lp.

Row 1 forward: Sk first vertical bar. *Tss in next vertical bar. Repeat from * across to final vertical bar. Tss into vertical bar and the horizontal bar behind it for stability. 46 lps on hook. Drop B.

Row 1 return: Switch to C by laying yarn on hook and starting to work with it.

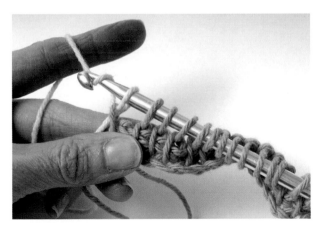

Yo, pull through 1 lp. *Yo, pull through 2 lps. Repeat from * until 1 lp remains on hook.

*Yo, pull through 2 lps. Repeat from * until 1 lp remains on hook.

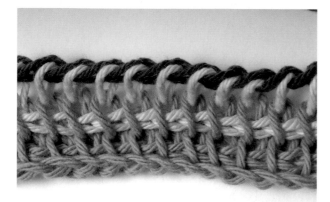

Row 2 forward: Repeat Row 1 forward. Drop C.

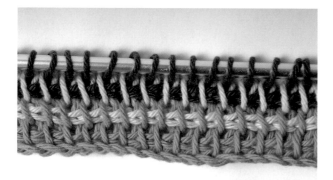

Row 2 return: With A, repeat Row 1 return.

Continue in pattern, working in same color for a return pass and then a forward pass. Switch to the next color at the beginning of the next return pass. Let the unused yarn hang to the back, picking it up in its turn. The last return row should be worked in A. Do not fasten off.

Edging

Insert hook in next vertical bar as for Tss. Yo, pull up lp. Yo, pull through 2 lps; sc made. Sc in each st across, 2 sc in corner (if this is too tight and makes corner curl up, work 3 sc in corner). Sc evenly down side and around rest of placemat to starting point. Join to first sc with sl st. Fasten off.

Dots and Dashes Placemat 1
(Blue and Yellow)

GAUGE

14 sts and 13 rows in pattern/4 inches (10 cm)

NOTE For gauge swatch, ch 21, then work in pattern until swatch measures at least 4 inches (10 cm).

With B, ch 41.

Foundation row forward: Insert hook in second ch from hook. Yo, pull up lp. Ch 1. *Insert hook in next ch, yo, pull up lp. Ch 1. Repeat from * across.

Foundation row return: Yo, pull through 1 lp. *Yo, pull through 2 lps. Repeat from * until 2 lps remain on hook.

NOTE You will change colors here, completing the final st of the return pass with D.

Drop B. Yo with D, pull through 2 lps.

Row 1 forward: Sk first vertical bar. Sl next vertical bar on hook.

NOTE Do not pull up lp, just sl the hook through the bar. It is almost like you are weaving the yarn back and forth.

from * across to final vertical bar. Work Tss in final vertical bar and the horizontal bar behind it for stability.

Row 3 return: As standard return. Do not change colors.

Row 4 forward: Sk first vertical bar. *Tss in next vertical bar. Repeat from * across to final vertical bar. Tss in final vertical bar and horizontal bar behind it for stability.

Row 4 return: As standard return until 2 lps remain on hook. Drop B, switch to D.

Repeat Rows 1–4 until placemat is desired size, ending with Row 4. Do not fasten off.

Edging

Insert hook in next vertical bar as for Tss. Yo, pull up lp. Yo, pull through 2 lps; sc made. Sc in each st across, 2 sc in corner (if this is too tight and makes corner curl up, work 3 sc in corner). Sc evenly down side and around rest of placemat to starting point. Join to first sc with sl st. Fasten off.

Dots and Dashes Placemat 2 (Purple and Yellow)

Work as for Dots and Dashes Placemat I, except substitute color C for color D.

*Bring yarn to front of work. Working behind the yarn, sl next vertical bar on hook.

Bring yarn to back of work. Working in front of the yarn, sl next vertical bar on hook. Repeat from * to final vertical bar. Tss in final vertical bar. Ch 1.

Row 1 return: As standard return. Do not change colors.

Row 2 forward: Sk first vertical bar. *Tss in next vertical bar. Repeat from * across to final vertical bar. Tss in final vertical bar and horizontal bar behind it for stability.

Row 2 return: As standard return until 2 lps remain on hook. Drop D, switch to B.

Row 3 forward: Sk first vertical bar. Bring yarn to front of work. Working behind the yarn, sl next vertical bar on hook. *Bring yarn to back of work. Working in front of yarn, sl next vertical bar on hook. Bring yarn to front of work. Working behind yarn sl next vertical bar on hook. Repeat

Four-Color Striped Placemat

Gauge

15 sts in Tunisian simple stitch/4 inches (10 cm); 16 rows in Tunisian simple stitch/5 inches (13 cm)

> **NOTE** For gauge swatch, ch 22, then continue in pattern until swatch measures at least 5 inches (13 cm).

> **NOTE** To achieve the four-color stripe pattern, you will switch colors at both ends.

With C, ch 46.

Foundation row forward: Insert hook in second ch from hook. Yo, pull up lp. *Insert hook in next ch. Yo, pull up lp. Each st adds another lp to the hook. Repeat from * across. Total 46 loops on hook. Drop C by letting it hang to back.

Foundation row return: Switch to A by laying yarn on hook and starting to work with it. Yo, pull through 1 lp. *Yo, pull through 2 lps. Repeat from * until 2 lps remain on hook. Drop A, switch to D. Complete final st of return pass with D.

Row 1 forward: Sk first vertical bar. With D, *Tss in next st. Repeat from * across to final vertical bar. Tss in final vertical bar and horizontal bar behind it for stability. Drop D.

Row 1 return: Switch to B by laying yarn on hook and starting to work with it. Yo, pull through 1 lp. *Yo, pull through 2 lps. Repeat from * until 2 lps remain on hook. Drop B, switch to A. Complete final st of return pass with A.

Repeat Row 1 forward and return in the following color pattern:

A forward, C return

B forward, D return
C forward, A return
D forward, B return

until placemat is desired size, ending with a return in color A, changing to D when 2 lps remain on hook.

Edging

With D, insert hook in next vertical bar as for Tss. Yo, pull up lp. Yo, pull through 2 lps; sc made. Sc in each st across, 2 sc in corner. (If this is too tight and makes corner curl up, work 3 sc in corner.) Sc evenly down side and around rest of placemat to starting point. Join to first sc with sl st. Fasten off.

Appendices

Standard Body Measurements/Sizing

Most crochet and knitting pattern instructions will provide general sizing information, such as the chest or bust measurements of a completed garment. Many patterns also include detailed schematics or line drawings. These drawings show specific garment measurements (bust/chest, neckline, back, waist, sleeve length, and so on) in all the different pattern sizes. To insure proper fit, always review all of the sizing information provided in a pattern before you begin.

Following are several sizing charts. These charts show Chest, Center Back Neck-to-Cuff, Back Waist Length, Cross Back, and Sleeve Length **actual body measurements** for babies, children, women, and men. These measurements are given in both inches and centimeters.

When sizing sweaters, the fit is based on actual chest/bust measurements, plus ease (additional inches or centimeters). The first chart entitled "Fit" recommends the amount of ease to add to body measurements if you prefer a close-fitting garment, an oversized garment, or something in-between.

The next charts provide average lengths for children's, women's and men's garments.

Both the Fit and Length charts are simply guidelines. For individual body differences, changes can be made in body and sleeve lengths when appropriate. However, consideration must be given to the project pattern. Certain sizing changes may alter the appearance of a garment.

HOW TO MEASURE

1. Chest/Bust
Measure around the fullest part of the chest/bust. Do not draw the tape too tightly.

2. Center Back Neck–to–Cuff
With arm slightly bent, measure from back base of neck across shoulder around bend of elbow to wrist.

3. Back Waist Length
Measure from the most prominent bone at base of neck to the natural waistline.

4. Cross Back
Measure from shoulder to shoulder.

5. Sleeve Length
With arm slightly bent, measure from armpit to cuff.

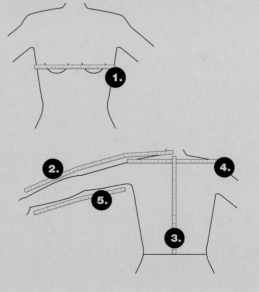

STANDARDS & GUIDELINES FOR CROCHET AND KNITTING

FIT

Very-close fitting: Actual chest/bust measurement or less
Close-fitting: 1–2"/2.5–5cm
Standard-fitting: 2–4"/5–10cm
Loose-fitting: 4–6"/10–15cm
Oversized: 6"/15cm or more

LENGTH FOR CHILDREN

Waist length: Actual body measurement
Hip length: 2"/5cm down from waist
Tunic length: 6"/15cm down from waist

LENGTH FOR WOMEN

Waist length: Actual body measurement
Hip length: 6"/15cm down from waist
Tunic length: 11"/28cm down from waist

LENGTH FOR MEN

Men's length usually varies only 1–2"/ 2.5–5cm from the actual "back hip length" measurement (*see chart*)

Baby's size	3 months	6 months	12 months	18 months	24 months
1. Chest (in.)	16	17	18	19	20
(cm.)	40.5	43	45.5	48	50.5
2. Center Back Neck-to-Cuff	10½	11½	12½	14	18
	26.5	29	31.5	35.5	45.5
3. Back Waist Length	6	7	7½	8	8½
	15.5	17.5	19	20.5	21.5
4. Cross Back (Shoulder to shoulder)	7¼	7¾	8¼	8½	8¾
	18.5	19.5	21	21.5	22
5. Sleeve Length to Underarm	6	6½	7½	8	8½
	15.5	16.5	19	20.5	21.5

Child's size	2	4	6	8	10
1. Chest (in.)	21	23	25	26½	28
(cm.)	53	58.5	63.5	67	71
2. Center Back Neck-to-Cuff	18	19½	20½	22	24
	45.5	49.5	52	56	61
3. Back Waist Length	8½	9½	10½	12½	14
	21.5	24	26.5	31.5	35.5
4. Cross Back (Shoulder to shoulder)	9¼	9¾	10¼	10¾	11¼
	23.5	25	26	27	28.5
5. Sleeve Length to Underarm	8½	10½	11½	12½	13½
	21.5	26.5	29	31.5	34.5

STANDARDS & GUIDELINES FOR CROCHET AND KNITTING

Child's (cont.)	12	14	16		
1. Chest (in.)	30	31½	32½		
(cm.)	*76*	*80*	*82.5*		
2. Center Back Neck-to-Cuff	26 / *66*	27 / *68.5*	28 / *71*		
3. Back Waist Length	15 / *38*	15½ / *39.5*	16 / *40.5*		
4. Cross Back (Shoulder to Shoulder)	12 / *30.5*	12¼ / *31*	13 / *33*		
5. Sleeve Length to Underarm	15 / *38*	16 / *40.5*	16½ / *42*		

Woman's size	X-Small	Small	Medium	Large	
1. Bust (in.)	28–30	32–34	36–38	40–42	
(cm.)	*71–76*	*81–86*	*91.5–96.5*	*101.5–106.5*	
2. Center Back Neck-to-Cuff	27–27½ / *68.5–70*	28–28½ / *71–72.5*	29–29½ / *73.5–75*	30–30½ / *76–77.5*	
3. Back Waist Length	16½ / *42*	17 / *43*	17¼ / *43.5*	17½ / *44.5*	
4. Cross Back (Shoulder to Shoulder)	14–14½ / *35.5–37*	14½–15 / *37–38*	16–16½ / *40.5–42*	17–17½ / *43–44.5*	
5. Sleeve Length to Underarm	16½ / *42*	17 / *43*	17 / *43*	17½ / *44.5*	

Woman's (cont.)	1X	2X	3X	4X	5X
1. Bust (in.)	44–46	48–50	52–54	56–58	60–62
(cm.)	*111.5–117*	*122–127*	*132–137*	*142–147*	*152–158*
2. Center Back Neck-to-Cuff	31–31½ / *78.5–80*	31½–32 / *80–81.5*	32½–33 / *82.5–84*	32½–33 / *82.5–84*	33–33½ / *84–85*
3. Back Waist Length	17¾ / *45*	18 / *45.5*	18 / *45.5*	18½ / *47*	18½ / *47*
4. Cross Back (Shoulder to Shoulder)	17½ / *44.5*	18 / *45.5*	18 / *45.5*	18½ / *47*	18½ / *47*
5. Sleeve Length to Underarm	17½ / *44.5*	18 / *45.5*	18 / *45.5*	18½ / *47*	18½ / *47*

STANDARDS & GUIDELINES FOR CROCHET AND KNITTING

Man's Size	Small	Medium	Large	X-Large	XX-Large
1. Chest (in.)	34–36	38–40	42–44	46–48	50–52
(cm.)	86–91.5	96.5–101.5	106.5–111.5	116.5–122	127–132
2. Center Back Neck-to-Cuff	32–32½	33–33½	34–34½	35–35½	36–36½
	81–82.5	83.5–85	86.5–87.5	89–90	91.5–92.5
3. Back Hip Length	25–25½	26½–26¾	27–27¼	27½–27¾	28–28½
	63.5–64.5	67.5–68	68.5–69	69.5–70.5	71–72.5
4. Cross Back (Shoulder to Shoulder)	15½–16	16½–17	17½–18	18–18½	18½–19
	39.5–40.5	42–43	44.5–45.5	45.5–47	47–48
5. Sleeve Length to Underarm	18	18½	19½	20	20½
	45.5	47	49.5	50.5	52

Head Circumference Chart

	Infant/Child				Adult	
	Premie	Baby	Toddler	Child	Woman	Man
6. Circumference (in.)	12	14	16	18	20	22
(cm.)	30.5	35.5	40.5	45.5	50.5	56

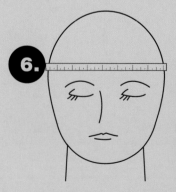

For an accurate head measure, place a tape measure across the forehead and measure around the full circumference of the head. Keep the tape snug for accurate results.

Standard Yarn Weight System

Categories of yarn, gauge ranges, and recommended needle and hook sizes

Yarn Weight Symbol & Category Names	1 Super Fine	2 Fine	3 Light	4 Medium	5 Bulky	6 Super Bulky
Type of Yarns in Category	Sock, Fingering, Baby	Sport, Baby	DK, Light Worsted	Worsted, Afghan, Aran	Chunky, Craft, Rug	Bulky, Roving
Knit Gauge Range* in Stockinette Stitch to 4 inches	27–32 sts	23–26 sts	21–24 sts	16–20 sts	12–15 sts	6–11 sts
Recommended Needle in Metric Size Range	2.25–3.25 mm	3.25–3.75 mm	3.75–4.5 mm	4.5–5.5 mm	5.5–8 mm	8 mm and larger
Recommended Needle U.S. Size Range	1 to 3	3 to 5	5 to 7	7 to 9	9 to 11	11 and larger
Crochet Gauge* Ranges in Single Crochet to 4 inch	21–32 sts	16–20 sts	12–17 sts	11–14 sts	8–11 sts	5–9 sts
Recommended Hook in Metric Size Range	2.25–3.5 mm	3.5–4.5 mm	4.5–5.5 mm	5.5–6.5 mm	6.5–9 mm	9 mm and larger
Recommended Hook U.S. Size Range	B–1 to E–4	E–4 to 7	7 to I–9	I–9 to K–10½	K–10½ to M–13	M–13 and larger

* GUIDELINES ONLY: The above reflect the most commonly used gauges and needle or hook sizes for specific yarn categories.

SKILL LEVELS FOR CROCHET

1	◖□□▭	**Beginner**	Projects for first-time crocheters using basic stitches. Minimal shaping.
2	◖■□▭	**Easy**	Projects using yarn with basic stitches, repetitive stitch patterns, simple color changes, and simple shaping and finishing.
3	◖■■▭	**Intermediate**	Projects using a variety of techniques, such as basic lace patterns or color patterns, mid-level shaping and finishing.
4	◖■■▶	**Experienced**	Projects with intricate stitch patterns, techniques and dimension, such as non-repeating patterns, multicolor techniques, fine threads, small hooks, detailed shaping and refined finishing.

This Standards & Guidelines booklet and downloadable symbol artwork are available at: **YarnStandards.com**

Resources

Books

Barnden, Betty. *The Crochet Stitch Bible.* Iola, WI: Krause Publications, 2004.

Christmas, Carolyn and Dorris Brooks. *101 Easy Tunisian Stitches.* Berne, IN: Annie's Attic, 2004.

Eckman, Edie. *The Crochet Answer Book.* North Adams, MA: Storey Publishing, 2005.

Matthews, Anne. *Vogue Dictionary of Crochet Stitches.* Newton, UK: David & Charles, 1987.

Reader's Digest. *The Ultimate Sourcebook of Knitting and Crochet Stitches.* Pleasantville, NY: Reader's Digest, 2003.

Silverman, Sharon Hernes. *Basic Crocheting.* Mechanicsburg, PA: Stackpole Books, 2006.

Silverman, Sharon Hernes. *Beyond Basic Crocheting.* Mechanicsburg, PA: Stackpole Books, 2007.

Magazines

Crochet!
www.crochetmagazine.com

Interweave Crochet
www.interweavecrochet.com

Vogue Knitting
www.vogueknitting.com

Recommended Designer Web Sites

Sharon Hernes Silverman
www.sharonsilverman.com

Kristin Omdahl
www.styledbykristin.com

NexStitch
www.nexstitch.com

Stitch Diva Studios
www.stitchdiva.com

Tunisian Hooks, Yarn, and Other Supplies

Your local yarn shop is the best source for supplies and advice. The staff is knowledgeable about yarns from many different manufacturers and can help you substitute one yarn for another or find just the right color combination. Questions are welcomed and advice is given freely. Check the shop's schedule for specialty classes to add to your skill set, and get on the mailing list so you can find out when your favorite yarn goes on sale.

Catalogs and online retailers sell yarn and equipment. Hundreds of providers exist; you can find them on the Internet by searching for "yarn," "crocheting," "Tunisian crochet hooks," or "free patterns." Here are just a few sources.

Blue Heron Yarns
www.blueheronyarns.com

Lion Brand Yarn Company
www.lionbrand.com

Louet North America
www.louet.com

Patternworks
www.patternworks.com

Plymouth Yarn Company, Inc.
www.plymouthyarn.com

Stitch Diva Studios (excellent source for hand-carved Tunisian hooks)
www.stitchdiva.com

Tahki • Stacy Charles, Inc.
www.tahkistacycharles.com

Unique Kolours/Colinette Yarns Ltd.
www.uniquekolours.com

Yarn Market
www.yarnmarket.com

Other Resources for Crocheters

CRAFT YARN COUNCIL OF AMERICA (CYCA)

The craft yarn industry's trade association has educational links and free projects.

www.craftyarncouncil.com

CROCHET GUILD OF AMERICA (CGOA)

The national association for crocheters, CGOA sponsors conventions, offers correspondence courses, and maintains a membership directory.

www.crochet.org

INTERWEAVE PRESS

Although more focused on knitting and other fiber arts than crocheting, Interweave does publish some excellent crochet books, and also publishes a special issue of their Interweave Knits magazine dedicated to crocheting.

www.interweave.com

THE NATIONAL NEEDLEARTS ASSOCIATION (TNNA)

This international trade organization represents retailers, manufacturers, distributors, designers, manufacturers' representatives, publishers, teachers, and wholesalers of products and supplies for the specialty needlearts market.

www.tnna.org

About the Author

PHOTO CREDIT—ALAN B. SILVERMAN

Sharon Hernes Silverman has been a freelance writer since 1987, concentrating on travel and crocheting. *Tunisian Crochet* is her twelfth book; she is also the author of several hundred newspaper and magazine articles.

Passionate about crocheting in general and Tunisian crochet in particular, Silverman is a professional member of the Crochet Guild of America and a design member of The National NeedleArts Association. She has appeared on several episodes of the fiber arts show "Uncommon Threads" on HGTV and the DIY Network. Silverman's designs have been featured by major yarn companies including Plymouth Yarn Company, Inc. and Louet North America. She teaches regularly at yarn shops and conferences, and invariably receives rave reviews for her classes.

Sharon Silverman lives with her husband and two sons in West Chester, Pennsylvania. To find out what's new, purchase patterns, get information about her teaching schedule, or contact her directly, please visit www.SharonSilverman.com.